Elisabetta Di Nitto · Peter Matthews
Dana Petcu · Arnor Solberg
Editors

Model-Driven Development and Operation of Multi-Cloud Applications

The MODAClouds Approach

Editors
Elisabetta Di Nitto
Politecnico di Milano
Milan
Italy

Peter Matthews
CA Technologies
Datchet, Berkshire
UK

Dana Petcu
Institute e-Austria
Western University of Timisoara
Timisoara
Romania

Arnor Solberg
SINTEF
Oslo
Norway

DOI 10.1007/978-3-319-46031-4

Library of Congress Control Number: 2016951966

Preface

In the last decade Cloud computing gained significant attention from both industrial and scientific communities. Despite the worldwide efforts to make it a utility service for anyone, the concept implementation still require specific IT skills. In this context, the book aims to present the approach undertaken to simplify the Cloud service usage process by the team of the European project named MODAClouds. The targeted audience are the developers and operators of the Cloud aware applications. More precisely, the undertaken approach is supporting the simplification of the cycle development-operation in multi-Cloud environments with a special emphasis on ensuring the quality of services.

This book covers a large number of topics related to development and operation in multi-Clouds and was designed to offer to its readers ideas on how to address the Development and Operation—*DevOps*—problems encountered when working with Cloud services. It is structured as follows:

- Chapter 1 introduces the problems faced by MODAClouds and provides a general overview of its approach.
- Chapters 2–4 are dedicated to the development (*Dev*) of multi-Cloud applications. In particular, Chap. 2 focuses on the approach for selecting a set of Cloud service offers by taking risks and costs into account, Chap. 3 focuses on the metamodels and on the tool supporting our model-driven development approach, and Chap. 4 on the way we support Quality of Service assessment as well as the management of Service Level Agreements.
- Chapters 5–8 are dedicated to the operation (*Ops*) of applications in a multi-Cloud context. More specifically, Chaps. 5 and 6 shortly present our multi-Cloud monitoring and load balancing mechanisms, respectively. Chapter 7 focuses on the way we support data migration and synchronization between different NoSQL Databases as a Service (DaaS). Finally, Chap. 8 focuses on the *supporting services* that enable the proper management of the MODAClouds runtime platform.
- Chapters 9–11 describe those features that enable integration between development and operation into a single *DevOps* framework. These include the usage

of the models@runtime paradigm for continuous design, deployment, operation and self-adaptation (Chap. 9), the way monitoring data from the operational environment are used at design time to support optimization of multi-Clouds applications (Chap. 10), and the best practices and design patterns we have identified to enable application DevOps in a multi-Cloud context (Chap. 11).

- Chapters 12–15 are dedicated to the presentation of the industrial cases we have adopted to evaluate and put in practice the MODAClouds approach. These cases concern different application domains and business needs. The first case is concerned with the development of collaborative Cloud-based features for a pre-existing, desktop-based UML case tool (Chap. 12), the second with a business process supporting system to be cloudified and optimized (Chap. 13), the third with an application to support care of patients with mental problems (Chap. 14). Finally, the fourth case describes how, from a research idea developed in the project, our partner infrastructure software provider has developed a specific technology that extends the features it offers to its users (Chap. 15). Three out of the four presented cases are now commercialized by the respective companies.
- Finally, Chap. 16 draws some conclusions and identify future research trends in the context of support to multi-Cloud applications development.

Acknowledgments Together with all authors of this book we are indebted to our advisory board members, Paola Inverardi, Parastoo Mohagheghi and Miguel Vidal, and to our reviewers for their constructive and useful suggestions. They have greatly helped us in shaping our project results. Also, we own gratitude to our project officer Lars Pedersen for his invaluable support through all phases of the project.

The work reported in this book is partially funded by the European Commission grant agreement number FP7-ICT-2011-8-318484 (MODAClouds). The MODAClouds project has been vital to the composition of this book and has been completed successfully with the end result of "excellent".

Milan, Italy	Elisabetta Di Nitto
Datchet, UK	Peter Matthews
Timisoara, Romania	Dana Petcu
Oslo, Norway	Arnor Solberg
June 2016	

Contents

Chapter 1
Introduction

Elisabetta Di Nitto and Dana Petcu

1.1 Context

Cloud computing is a major trend in the ICT industry. The wide spectrum of available Clouds, such as those offered by Microsoft, Google, Amazon, HP, AT&T, and IBM, just to mention big players, provides a vibrant technical environment, where even small and medium enterprises (SMEs) use cheap and flexible services creating innovative solutions and evolving their existing service offer. Despite this richness of environments, Cloud business models and technologies are characterized by critical issues, such as the heterogeneity between vendor technologies and the resulting **lack of interoperability** between Clouds. In this setting a number of challenges for systems developers and operators can be identified, especially for SMEs that have limited resources and do not have the strength to influence the market. In particular:

- **Vendor Lock-in** [1, 2]. Cloud providers offer proprietary solutions that force Cloud customers to decide, at the early stages of software development the design and deployment models to adopt (e.g., public vs. hybrid Clouds) as well as the technology stack (e.g., Amazon Simple DB vs. Google Bigtable).
- **Risk Management**. There are several concerns when selecting a Cloud technology such as payment models, security, legal and contractual, quality and integration with the enterprise architecture and culture.

E. Di Nitto (✉)
Politecnico di Milano - DEIB, Piazza L. da Vinci, 32, 20133 Milan, Italy
e-mail: elisabetta.dinitto@polimi.it

D. Petcu (✉)
Institute e-Austria TimiŞoara and West University of TimiŞoara,
B-dul Vasile Pârvan 4, 300223 TimiŞoara, Romania
e-mail: petcu@info.uvt.ro

E. Di Nitto et al. (eds.), *Model-Driven Development and Operation of Multi-Cloud Applications*, PoliMI SpringerBriefs,
DOI 10.1007/978-3-319-46031-4_1

- **Quality Assurance**. Cloud performance can vary at any point in time. Elasticity may not ramp at desired speeds. Unavailability problems exist even when 99.9 % up-time is advertised (e.g., Amazon EC2 and Microsoft Office 365 outages in 2011).

The above issues can be addressed by enabling companies to develop their applications for multiple Cloud targets, by offering them proper tools to analyze the risks, performance and cost of various solutions and identify the ones that best suit the needs of the specific case, and by supporting a multi-Cloud deployment of applications to ensure a level of availability that is greater than the one offered by each specific Cloud. In this context, within the MODAClouds project, we focused on the following objectives:

- Deliver an advanced software engineering model-driven approach and an Integrated Development Environment (IDE) to support systems developers in building and deploying applications, together with related data, to multi-Clouds spanning across the full Cloud stack (Infrastructure as a Service, shortly IaaS, Platform as a Service, shortly PaaS, and Software as a Service, shortly SaaS).
- Define quality measures, monitoring mechanisms, prediction models, and adaptive policies to provide quality assurance in Clouds and multi-Clouds.
- Provide support to costs and risks analysis to increase trust in Clouds.
- Develop an integration framework between design tools and run-time.
- Create relevant and complex case studies for the entire risks assessment and software engineering methodologies.
- Analyze and validate project outcomes through case studies.
- Ensure distribution of project results via dissemination activities on relevant publication channels, training, and standardization.
- Provide community-based open source solutions supporting the full applications life-cycle.

In this chapter we provide a motivation for the adoption of a multi-Cloud approach and of a model-driven, quality aware development and operation paradigm (Sect. 1.2), offer a brief overview of related work (Sect. 1.3), introduce the MODAClouds approach and toolset (Sects. 1.4 and 1.5), and, finally, define the goals of this book (Sect. 1.6).

1.2 Motivation

The main drivers for exploiting a multiple Cloud approach can be of various nature, from the need to avoid dependence from a single provider to the need to follow local constraints and laws, to the opportunity to replicate software in order to enhance availability. The main factors we have identified are summarized in Fig. 1.1. In the figure we distinguish between those drives that imply the simultaneous usage of services from multiple Clouds and those that are more concerned with the possibility

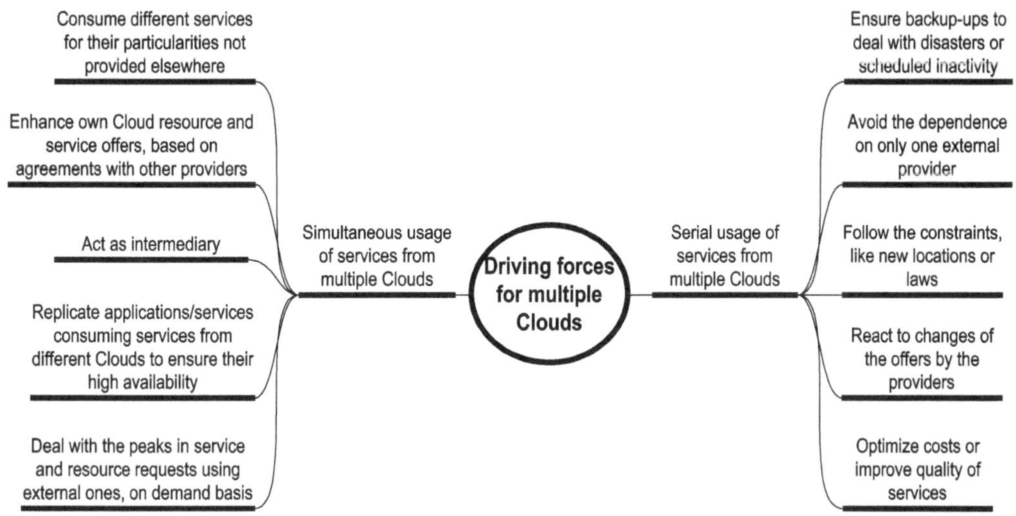

Fig. 1.1 Drivers for multi-Cloud adoption

of preparing a software system to be run on multiple Clouds but still using a single Cloud at a time during operation.

To exemplify concrete needs in an industrial context, we refer to the case of a small company that we call MODAFIN, specialised in IT applications for financial services. Its main product line is a proprietary solution for stock market operations, cash administration, and lending management.

MODAFIN most profitable activities are software customization and life-cycle management for this product line.

Customisation involves development of custom modules to accommodate new functional requirements. Moreover, it includes application integration with existing databases and legacy business systems at the customer' site.

Life-cycle management needs to assure high-availability for real-time computations during market hours, scalability and low operational costs for batch analytic workloads running after-hours. MODAFIN fulfills these quality requirements with a capacity management consultancy team following the application life-cycle.

The consultancy team has been working for a long time at the customers' site, where the system is deployed in the operation environment. Thanks to the diffusion of the Cloud, however, new needs have arisen. At night, some customers want to run their batch analytic workloads at the cheapest operational costs of Amazon on-spot instances. During the day, they expect calculation engines to ramp-up computing power at an unprecedented pace when the stock market gets volatile. Moreover, some customer applications are collecting and processing stock market data directly on the Cloud using PaaS datastore services such as Google Bigtable or Amazon SimpleDB. At the same time, customers are cutting spending in consultancy services for life-cycle management as they are relying more and more on SaaS services.

To remain competitive, MODAFIN solution must evolve addressing all above requirements. To do so, the Company needs to apply advanced software engineering methodologies revising both the software development process and its life-cycle management services:

- It needs to develop a solution that can be executed on a broad spectrum of customers IaaS/PaaS, also supporting Cloud bursting, that is, the ability to move part of the system on a different Cloud to manage pick of traffic when needed.
- It must develop a flexible architecture for the system so that it could be adapted to new Cloud offers emerging in the next 5–10 years to adapt to changes of context and requirements.
- It needs libraries and connectors to integrate various data storage tools and services to address different needs in terms of performance, data locality, scalability and the like.
- It needs simple to use tools to perform what if analyses and optimizations on the system configuration in order to allow for the fulfillment of the required QoS.
- It needs a multi-Cloud environment for execution, which supports monitoring, smart load balancing, scale-in and out on several Clouds to avoid that availability or performance outages of a single Cloud provider would turn into a disaster for MODAFIN's own business.

All above needs result not only in the adoption of a multi-cloud approach, but also in the exploitation of a proper development and operation set of tools and methods, which are specifically built to support multi-Cloud.

Within the MODAClouds approach we have experimented with model-driven development enhanced with the possibility of exploiting models not only as part of design but also as part of the runtime. In this case the system model becomes a live object that evolves with the system itself and can be used to send back to the design time powerful information that enables a continuous improvement of the system. In new terms, this approach goes into the direction of offering a valid tool to support DevOps, that is, the ability to support development and operation in a seamless way.

1.3 Related Work

Model-driven engineering (MDE) allows developers to build the system at various level of abstractions. It is often summarized as "model once, generate anywhere" and, as such, becomes particularly relevant when it comes to provisioning and deployment of applications and services across multiple Clouds, as well to migration of source code and data from one service provider to another.

Services Oriented Architecture (SOA) related technologies are often used to define Cloud-enabled applications without going into the fine details of deployment. Services are often modeled by means of general purpose languages such as UML. Service-specific languages have also been designed for SOA approach (e.g. SoaML[1]). USDL[2] goes even further, by allowing designers to specify, beside services and their

[1]http://www.omg.org/spec/SoaML/1.0/Beta2/.

[2]http://www.w3.org/2005/Incubator/usdl/.

interfaces, non-functional aspects of these services (e.g. pricing, legal, certification, documentation).

Other approaches are related to the specific concept of Web Service: WSDL[3] enables the specification of a list of services, interfaces, data types and orchestration processes at a syntactical level, OWL[4] is a semantic Web language which enables the specification of the semantics of the services, besides their syntax. Both these approaches do not allow for the description of non-functional requirements and constraints. However, they can be complemented with the OMG UML profile for QoS, QFTP,[5] which allows a designer to specify QoS requirements and to connect them to service descriptions.

While the above approaches are Cloud-agnostic, modeling concepts and technologies for supporting provisioning, deployment and adaptation of applications in the Cloud have been recently developed. They exploit the uniform interfaces provided by various libraries for application deployment and control at run-time. We can mention here the most successful ones: jclouds,[6] libcloud,[7] δ-cloud[8] or fog.[9] For example, the jclouds model includes the description of nodes with metadata (like CPU, RAM, security policy), parameters (like minCPU, OS type) and a set of commands to be executed on nodes, as well as on the groups of nodes to be managed together.

Most of the above mentioned libraries are providing a common access to multiple Clouds, but are dependent on the programming language. Typically, they provide a code-based model of the infrastructure and do not offer any mechanism for automatic provisioning and deployment of applications on the Clouds. Moreover, they work at the IaaS level and do not expect applications and services to be presented in terms of models. To fill this gap, MODAClouds offers a complete set of model-based tools from design to deployment and run-time control of the applications.

Recently, several frameworks for managing multi-Cloud services and applications have been developed. They provide capabilities for the provisioning, deployment, monitoring, and adaptation of applications without being language-dependent. We mention here three of them: Cloudify,[10] Scalr[11] and CloudFoundry.[12] For example, the Cloudify model for deploying applications includes recipes for information like: (i) required infrastructure and how it should be used, (ii) clusters of service instances that make up an application tier, (iii) configuration (including provisioning and scaling rules) of an application and the services it is made of, (iv) probes used to monitor the status of the system. These frameworks are important to optimise performance,

---

[3] http://www.w3.org/TR/wsdl.

[4] http://www.w3.org/Submission/2004/SUBM-OWL-S-20041122/.

[5] http://www.omg.org/spec/QFTP/.

[6] http://jclouds.apache.org.

[7] http://libcloud.apache.org.

[8] http://deltacloud.apache.org.

[9] http://fog.io.

[10] http://www.cloudify.org.

[11] http://scalr.com.

[12] http://www.cloudfoundry.org.

availability, and cost of multi-Cloud systems. However, they do not come with any structured guideline/methodology, thus, developers and operators are typically left hacking at code level rather than engineering multi-Cloud systems following a structured tool-supported methodology.

The models@runtime paradigm, often used in MDE, proposes to leverage models during the execution of adaptive software systems to monitor and control the way they adapt. This approach enables the continuous evolution of the system with no strict boundaries between design-time and runtime activities. Models@runtime provides an abstract representation of the running system causally connected to the underlying state of the system which facilitates reasoning, simulation and enactment of adaptation actions. A change in the running system is automatically reflected in a model of the current system. A modification applied to this model can be enacted on the running system on demand. Thanks to the use of models, well-defined interface are provided to monitor the system and adapt it. The models also provide a way to measure the impact of changes in the system and analyse them before their enactment on the running system. In MODAClouds we adopt the models@runtime concept in order to tame the complexity of adaptation and ease the reasoning process for self-adaptation.

MODAClouds was developed together with two siblings projects, PaaSage and ARTIST. The scope of PaaSage[13] was to extend application models with annotations concerning platform and user's goals and preference. The language used for this is called Cloud Application Modelling and Execution Language (CAMEL). CAMEL integrates various domain-specific languages using the Eclipse Modelling Framework. Within this context, PaaSage has extend and adapt MODAClouds' CloudML to support model-based provisioning and deployment of Cloud-based systems. CloudML is used also by the ARTIST initiative,[14] which offers a set of methods and tools for an end-to-end assisted migration of legacy software to the Cloud. ARTIST followed an earlier initiative, REMICS[15] which proposed a leap progress in legacy systems migration to Service Clouds by providing a model driven methodology and tool following the Architecture Driven Modernization concept (use knowledge discovery to recover application models and rebuild the applications following the discovered models).

The MONDO initiative[16] focused not on MDE for Clouds, but on Clouds for MDE: aiming to achieve scalability in MDE, MONDO provided an integrated open-source and Cloud-based platform for scalable model persistence, indexing and retrieval facilities, support for collaborative modelling, and parallel execution of model queries and transformations, and an Eclipse-based developer workbench that include tooling for developing queries and transformations, for querying model indexes, and for constructing large models and domain specific languages. The HEADS initiative.[17]

[13] http://www.passage.eu.

[14] http://www.artist-project.eu.

[15] http://www.remics.eu.

[16] http://www.mondo-project.org.

[17] http://www.heads-project.eu.

leveraged MDE to provide an open-source Integrated Development Environment (IDE) supporting the collaboration between platform experts (platform for mobile devices, sensors, smart objects, etc.) and Cloud-based service developers and including a domain specific modeling language and a methodology for the specification, validation, deployment and evolution of software-intensive services distributed across the future computing continuum (composed of a wide set of heterogeneous platforms).

1.4 The MODAClouds Approach

Figure 1.2 shows an overview of the MODAClouds development approach. In particular, it shows how an application is designed and packaged for deployment according to a Cloud-tailored model-driven approach. Software designers start from defining the application structure and the corresponding Quality of Service (QoS) requirements at the *Cloud Independent Model* level (CIM). In the example shown in the figure, the application is composed of three components, two of which are further decomposed in sub-components. Availability and response time requirements are defined and associated to two of the application components. At this level there is no reference to specific Cloud services and resources as the focus is exclusively on the high level design of the application itself.

From the CIM level description the designer moves then to focus on introducing Cloud-specific aspects at the *Cloud-Provider Independent Model* level (CPIM). At this level, he/she may decide, for instance, to select a certain class of database service (e.g., key-value NoSQL) and certain kinds of computational and memory resources. All these are then associated to the application logic elements they contribute to realize. At this point the developer can start running the MODAClouds QoS analysis tool that, based on the defined QoS requirements and on the typical characteristics of the selected kinds of Cloud resources and services, can provide some feedback about the realizability of the application on specific Clouds and can suggest possible optimizations.

As soon as the designer is satisfied with the specified solution, he/she can move to the *Cloud-Provider Independent Model* level (CPSM) from where he/she can finalize the selection of specific providers and services/resources for the application, run more precise QoS analyses and, finally, generate proper deployment, monitoring and self-adaptation scripts to support the runtime phases.

In all analysis and design phases, the application designers as well as the decision makers from the company can be supported in the definition of risks and benefits for the application and in the identification of the candidate Cloud services and resources based on these.

Finally, at runtime, the models defined at design time are exploited to monitor and manage the application by enabling smart self-adaptation. Moreover, the values of specific metrics characteristic for the running applications are collected and passed to the development team that can exploit them to fine-tune the application.

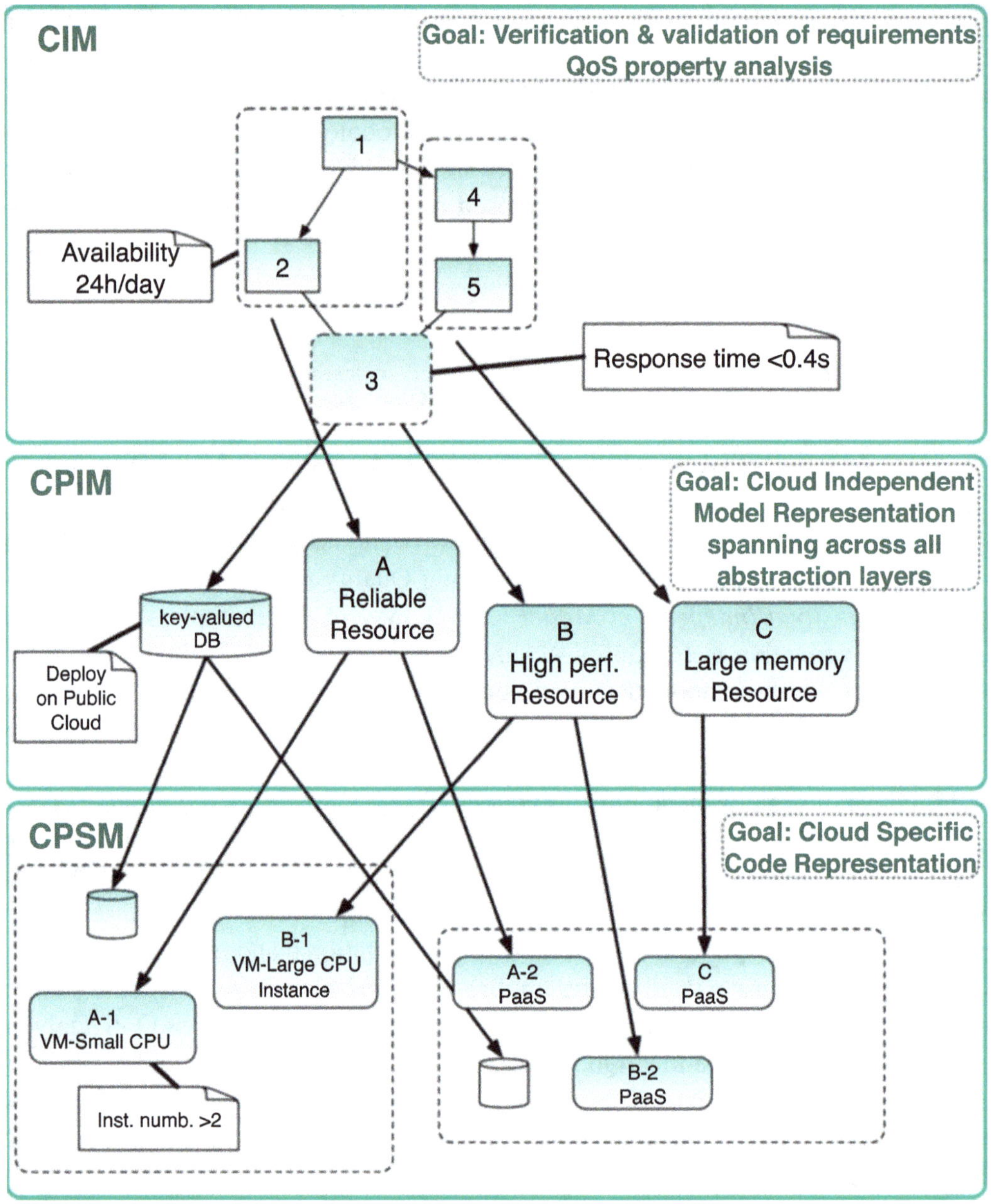

Fig. 1.2 Model-driven development in MODAClouds

As described in Chap. 10, this enables the adoption of a DevOps approach [3] that supports development and operation in a coherent manner.

1.5 The MODAClouds Toolbox

The MODAClouds model-driven approach is supported by the MODAClouds Toolbox (see Fig. 1.3). The toolbox helps lowering existing barriers between Development and Operations Teams and helps embracing DevOps practices within IT teams.

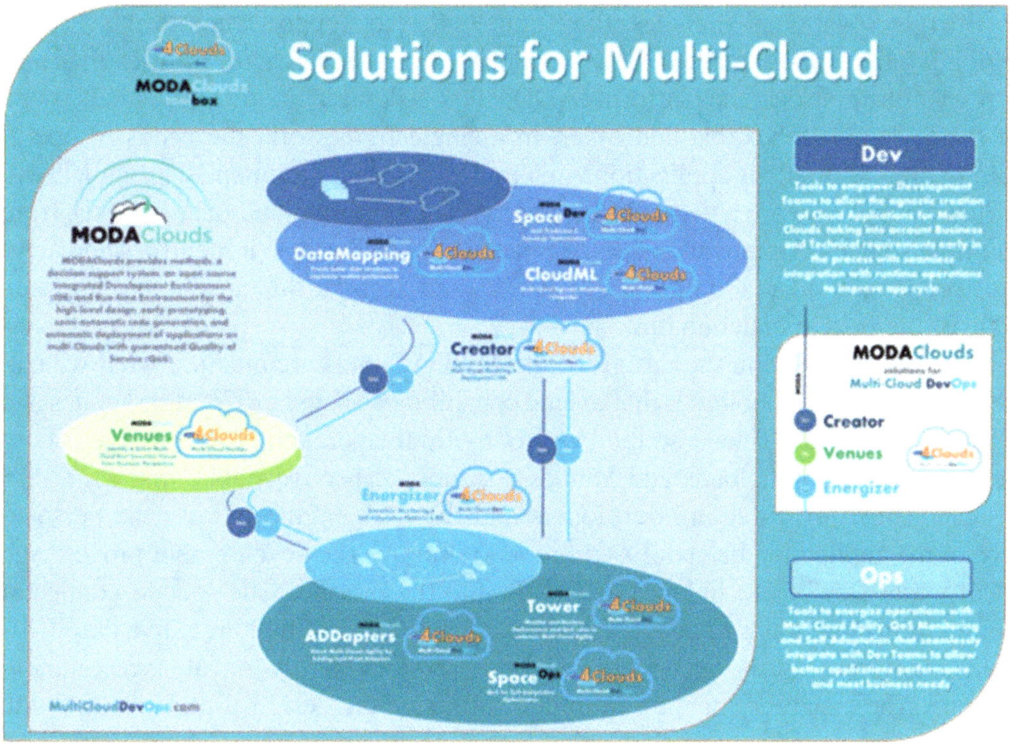

Fig. 1.3 MODAClouds toolbox

Thanks to it, organizations of any size can Build and Run Cloud Applications driven by business and technical needs and quality requirements. The toolbox is comprised of the following elements: (1) *Creator 4Clouds*, an Integrated Development Environment (IDE) for high-level application design; (2) *Venues 4Clouds*, a decision support system that helps decision makers identify and select the best execution venue for Cloud applications, by considering technical and business requirements; (3) *Energizer 4Clouds*, a Multi-Cloud Run-time Environment energized to provide automatic deployment and execution of applications with guaranteed Quality of Service (QoS) on compatible Multi-Clouds.[18]

Creator 4Clouds, in turn, includes plugins focusing on (i) analysing the QoS/cost trade-offs of various possible application configurations (Space 4Clouds^{Dev}), (ii) mapping high level data models into less expressive but more scalable NoSQL, (iii) deploying the resulting application on multi-Cloud by exploiting the CloudML language. Overall, Creator 4Clouds is a unique tool supporting design, development, deployment and resource provisioning for multi-Cloud applications. It limits lock-in and provides features to assess the QoS guarantees required by the application. Moreover, it offers support to the definition of the application SLA.

[18] All these tools are available as open source, see http://www.modaclouds.eu/software/.

Energizer 4Clouds includes the frameworks to support monitoring (Tower 4Clouds) and self-adaptation (Space 4Clouds^{Ops}), together with utilities that perform ancillary tasks in the platform (ADDapters 4Clouds). Energizer 4Clouds is one of the few approaches that addresses, in a single framework, the needs of operators willing to run their applications in a multi-Cloud environment. Through Tower 4Clouds, operators are able to perform complex monitoring and data analyses from multiple sources. Moreover, thanks to Space 4Clouds for Ops, it identifies and actuates proper self-adaptation actions that take into account the current and foreseen state of the system under control.

We have included in the design of the MODAClouds architecture what we call *Feed-Back Loop* technologies that extend capabilities offered by Creator, Venues and Energizer 4Clouds. Thanks to the Feed-Back Loop approach, Tower 4Clouds connects with Creator 4Clouds and Venues 4Clouds, respectively. The first connector is responsible for providing developers and the QoS engineers with the perspective of the application behavior at runtime to improve the development process and incorporate DevOps techniques and tools into the process. The second connector allows Venues 4Clouds to adapt its knowledge base according to real live data. This helps in offering to users an updated vision of services quality for future recommendations. The capability of the runtime to influence the design time is in line with current research and is a very important feature to empower multi-Cloud application developers.

1.6 Book Objectives

The objective of this book is to: (i) present the methods and tools composing the MODAClouds solution as well as the business needs they address, and (ii) to show their validity and utility through four industrial cases. The presentation will highlight both development and operation aspects and the way they are integrated to support a DevOps approach.

References

1. Gartner (2012) 2012 Cloud Computing Planning Guide
2. Forbes (2011) Cloud computing's vendor lock-in problem: why the industry is taking a step backward
3. Debois P (2011) DevOps: a software revolution in the making? J Inf Technol Manage

Chapter 2
Cloud Service Offer Selection

Smrati Gupta, Peter Matthews, Victor Muntés-Mulero and Jacek Dominiak

2.1 Introduction: Selecting Services for Agile Application Development

In the application economy, digital business initiatives are at the forefront of the growth strategy of many companies. Cloud based solutions offer a significant competitive advantage for both large companies and SMEs, leading to a rapid increase in the number of Cloud Service Providers (CSP). An important CSP driver is the improvement of consumers' experience through digital platforms that allow users to access data and services from any location and through multiple channels with assured performance and availability. This is usually studied from a single provider perspective, ignoring the growing number of multi-Cloud applications that use different Cloud services from different Cloud service providers. Beyond the usual Cloud services and providers, the interest in the Internet of Things (IoT) and fog computing is growing very fast as it is seen as an opportunity to launch innovative new services in the very near future. With the market growth and the increase in the number of components and applications in modern systems, the complexity of software systems implemented in multi-Cloud environments increases exponentially. Making decisions in the new era of multi-Cloud applications becomes one of the next challenges.

S. Gupta · V. Muntés-Mulero · J. Dominiak
CA Technologies Spain, 08940 Cornellà de Llobregat, Barcelona, Spain
e-mail: smrati.gupta@ca.com

V. Muntés-Mulero
e-mail: victor.muntes@ca.com

J. Dominiak
e-mail: jacek.dominiak@ca.com

P. Matthews (✉)
CA Technologies UK, Ditton Park, Riding Court Road, Datchet SL3 9LL, UK
e-mail: peter.matthews@ca.com

E. Di Nitto et al. (eds.), *Model-Driven Development and Operation of Multi-Cloud Applications*, PoliMI SpringerBriefs,
DOI 10.1007/978-3-319-46031-4_2

Software companies need to work through fast innovation cycles to be competitive in a changing and dynamic market. Following continuous delivery approaches becomes essential, increasing the need for agile decisions. Analogous to many other IT platforms, multi-Cloud applications (see Part IV) face important challenges related to security, availability, performance, compliance, integration, purchasing, automation and insight. Selecting the best Cloud service for a particular application requires an understanding of application requirements, and the interoperability between this specific service and other services offered by other CSP used by the application. This decision may have an important impact not only on the performance and user experience of the application and through them the business support. As the role of the CIO becomes that of an orchestrator of these increasingly complex systems, decisions do not depend anymore on a single dimension or a single person. The best service selection depends on multiple criteria including at least cost, risk and quality. Fast iterations in continuous delivery models require involving different stakeholders in the system, providing complementary perspectives, including for instance business decision makers, architects and systems operators. One of the main challenges is to find an efficient mechanism that allows translating these requirements into measurable metrics that make it possible to evaluate the fitness of a particular set of Cloud services and providers for a particular application. In this chapter, we discuss Decision Support Systems (DSS) for Cloud service selection. We discuss the main challenges related to DSS and present the tools implemented for this purpose. Afterward, we discuss the evolution of these DSS in the future and discuss next steps.

2.2 Decision Support System for Cloud Service Selection

The development of a recommendation system to assist the Cloud service selection is an interesting challenge from both conceptual and technical point of view. In this section, we highlight the major challenges that are required to be addressed in development of a generic decision support system that assists the Cloud service selection process from heterogeneous nature of services in Multi-Cloud environment.

Cloud Service Selection for Continuous Delivery

Continuous delivery is a frequently mentioned goal for IT departments. The emergence of apps on a smart phone has driven a move from the traditional waterfall method of development to the agile development strategy. Agile development has moved the application deployment bottleneck from development to operations and DevOps is a process that will remove the bottleneck to continuous delivery. This has been shown to deliver apps that are constantly refreshed with new features and fixes at a decreased cost and higher velocity. Delivering new applications requires speed and flexibility and is facilitated by creating applications from components such as Cloud services. Composing services into new applications reduces the amount of new developed code that needs to be written. As such there is little to check into a configuration and source code management environment beyond the links to services and workflow. The challenge is in selection of services that match the functionality required without sacrifice of performance and availability.

Risk Analysis for Cloud Service Selection in Multi-Clouds

A decision support system for Cloud service selection requires a systematic mechanism to allow the translation of the requirements of the naÏve users into tangible properties of the Cloud services that need to be assessed while making a selection. Furthermore, the mechanism needs to ensure provision of quality guarantees as desired by the end users. Risk Analysis provides a solution for development of such a mechanism. The existence of relevant risks poses a complex problem in selection and adoption of appropriate Cloud services. Consequently, identification, definition and quantification of these risks are important considerations in decision support system development.

Another advantage of adopting risk based analysis in decision support design for Cloud service selection is the integration of multiple stakeholders into the decision-making process. Risk analysis provides a concrete method of translating the requirements from multiple stakeholders involved in the decision making process into the properties of Cloud services in the desired domains.

Risk based analysis provides a mechanism to systematically analyze the quality of Cloud services by assessing the risks they impose on the critical domains and the Cloud service properties that can mitigate those risks, underpinning the satisfaction of quality requirements.

The first step in risk based analysis involves identification of risks in Cloud service selection. A common method of identifying risks is to allow the users to present their requirements in terms of the assets they intend to protect. Assets can be described as business oriented or technical, tangible or intangible, etc. The risks that the user entails by "cloudifying" its assets can be then be systematically determined. Some typical risks in multiple Cloud domains are:

- Unauthorized Access from IaaS Provider
- Insufficient Isolation
- Insufficient Physical Security
- Data Exposure to Government Authorities
- Increase of infrastructure prices
- Expensive support services
- Change of Price models
- Storage System Corruption

Risks can be mitigated by using Cloud services that have properties that ensure mitigation of those risks. For example, mitigating properties can be the existence of sufficient support services, data location in desirable geographical boundaries, sufficient certifications from the Cloud service providers, financial stability conditions, etc. In general, these properties are treatments for risks such that they ensure mitigation. The risk based analysis provides a mapping of user requirements defined as assets into desirable Cloud properties described as treatments within a decision support system.

There are additional risks associated with multi-Cloud environment service selection. Such risks can include vendor lock-in, complex data migration, interoperability, security breaches, cost unpredictability etc. These risks require some additional properties to be satisfied in order to mitigate them. These properties are not essentially associated with the Cloud service, but with the interaction between the services. For example, as a user may select services from different providers, he faces the risk of the interoperability between the services due to compatibility issues, SLA issues, or simple change in price models of a certain service leveraging affect on other services. Such risks are mitigated by imposing constraints on the selection of a set of services rather than a single service.

Risk based analysis provides a means of communicating user requirements in a decision support system development. It also provides a mechanism for quality assessment and identification of comparative domains among the different services in single Cloud and multi-Cloud environment.

2.3 Cloud Service Description Standardization

The standardisation activity relating to service description has been very patchy and incomplete. A form of service description using common data types and structures is a precursor to service matchmaking decisions. There have been a variety of service descriptions and standardisation efforts over the years but few, it any have had any lasting impact.

One of these efforts that had initial promise was the Service Measurement Index (SMI) [1]. SMI was an initiative started by CA Technologies and later adopted by Carnegie Mellon University who managed the Cloud Services Measurement Index Consortium (CSMIC).[1] SMI was based on a theory of "relative goodness" which was used to circumvent the more accurate but complex semantic solutions for comparison. SMI was finally abandoned when filling even a small portion of the database for describing services proved problematical. The approach taken by MODAClouds has been to use data that provides constraints or functional and non-functional requirements and pragmatically evaluating that data for gathering based on the method of gathering and the availability of the data. The MODAClouds project felt that there was little point in mandating a metric that could not be gathered or relied on the good will and compliance of a wide number of CSPs. Data acquisition is an on-going limitation to the description and comparison of Cloud services.

2.4 Data Gathering in Multi-Cloud Environments

The quality of recommendations made by the DSS is heavily dependent on the quality of data used for comparison of Cloud services. Quality data enhances the possibility of meeting requirements of the users more closely, but also provides the users more

[1] https://slate.adobe.com/a/PN39b/.

dimensions to compare the Cloud services in. Data gathering for comparison has a number of obstacles:

- *Lack of interest or business value*: CSPs are the primary source of data about the Cloud services. Small CSPs may enter data into a DSS database as a potential dissemination strategy. Larger CSPs such as Amazon have no incentive to provide comparison data and indeed expressly exclude the possibility in their terms and conditions.
- *Legal issues and accuracy from third party portals*: There are multiple analytic portals (e.g. CloudHarmony, Cloudymetrics etc.) that provide a comparative analysis of different Cloud services. Data from these websites can be accessed through APIs or simple parsing etc. However, this incurs a risk of data accuracy being dependant on a the third party. Legal constraints such as copyright and terms and conditions may also prevent the use of third party data.
- *Crowdsourced data quality*: Another mechanism to gather data regarding Cloud services is via crowdsourcing. Data provision by individuals is subject to the same accuracy and subjective opinions as travel recommendation and review sites.
- *Procurement Complexity*: Common complexity of the data gathering process from the technical perspective is that parsed data may not follow any commonly known structure. The most valuable data for comparison purposes is often described in free hand fashion such as reviews or articles.
- *Lack of standards*: Another example of the problem within the data gathering process is lack of clear JSON based standard or lack of validating structure, which is the base of XML.

Data gathering is an integral component to decision support and the module must provide a mechanism to automatically gather and update data ensuring its accuracy and currency.

2.5 Coping with Complexity in SaaS

An important consideration in the development of a DSS is the clear identification of the paradigms of comparison among the different Cloud services. Risk based analysis provides a systematic procedure for defining the requirements for Cloud services, but still creates a challenge to build a clear paradigm of comparison for Software as a Service (SaaS). IaaS and PaaS domains are more simple due to the objective nature of paradigms (comparison based on technical specifications, based on nature of platforms etc.). SaaS domains implies a higher user interaction thereby providing a more abstract quantification of paradigms to compare them with. In addition, the types of SaaS is highly varied and lacks any bench-marking and standardization. Therefore, for a DSS development, it is highly complex to provide recommendation for SaaS domain. It is crucial to take into account this complexity for the design of a multi-Cloud DSS.

2.6 Decision Support Tools for Cloud Service Selection

In order to address the challenges outlined in the previous section, the MODAClouds DSS was developed as a generic recommendation system that provides assistance in Cloud service selection taking into account the multi-Cloud environment and heterogeneous domains of the services. The DSS prototype is based on a risk analysis based requirement generation allowing multiple stakeholder participation along with inherent data gathering mechanisms and provides recommendations by solving the multi-criteria decision making problem. In this section, we outline the conceptual backbone forming the DSS.

The basic building blocks of DSS are comprised of three main processes: first, data gathering and evaluation from the end user; second, data gathering and evaluation from the Cloud service providers, and third, service matchmaking (see Fig. 2.1). The primary step is to assimilate data from end users and process it in order to identify end user requirements. In addition, there is a requirement to gather the data about the Cloud services and their providers (directly or using third party services e.g., websites which provide comparative analysis of Cloud service provider), and evaluate it. Finally, there is a need for service matchmaking, where the processed data from Cloud service providers is fine-tuned or operated upon by the end-user requirements to generate appropriate solutions. A major challenge identified in the decision making process is the specification of the requirements from the end user. To overcome this challenge, the proposed DSS assists users in specifying their requirements by enabling them to define the assets-risk-treatments. The end user can be the business decision maker, technical system architect, risk analyst and requirements engineer in an enterprise. End users are required to specify assets that they intend to protect. These assets can be intangible or tangible. Intangible assets are further subdivided as business oriented or technical oriented assets. Typical examples of business oriented intangible assets (BSOIA) include customer loyalty, product innovation, sales rate, etc. Similarly, typical examples of technical oriented intangible assets (TOIA) include data integrity, service availability, end user performance, etc. Furthermore,

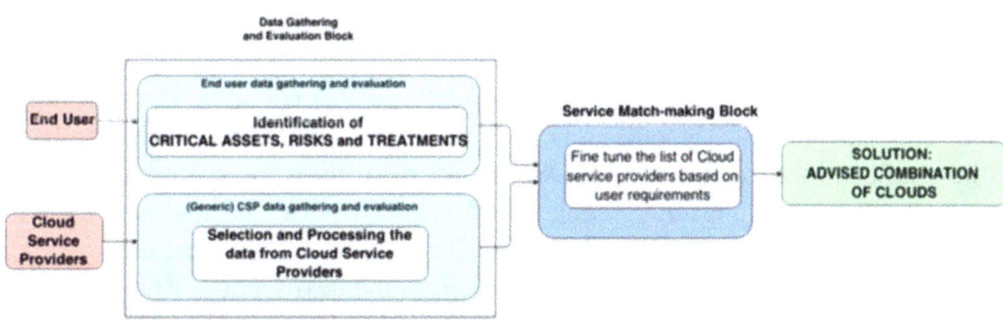

Fig. 2.1 Basic Building Blocks of DSS

the system architect is also allowed to specify the tangible assets which require to be protected in order to protect the business and technical oriented intangible assets. The tangible assets describe the architectural elements that are intended to be externalized using the Cloud services. Typical examples of such assets includes server (IaaS), database (PaaS), Middleware (SaaS), etc. Along with this specification, the end-user is expected to supply the 'importance' of an asset on a risk acceptability scale which identifies how much risk can a tangible asset endure.

Each of the assets supplied by the end user, is susceptible to certain risks. Therefore, the DSS allows the users to map the possible risks from which the asset needs to be protected. The identification of these risks per asset is a progressive learning process. The risks associated with different assets are identified with each use of the DSS, and are stored in the database. As the number of DSS users increases, the association of assets to risks becomes richer and more concrete.

Identifying the risks per asset, the user also identifies the likelihood and consequence of each risk, communicating the impact that is associated with each risk on the asset to the DSS. The scales of expressing these quantities are:

- Likelihood: rare (1), unlikely (2), possible (3), likely (4), certain (5)
- Consequence: insignificant (1), minor (2), moderate (3), major (4), catastrophic (5)

A joint function quantifies the risk from the inputs above. This function is highly flexible in nature: it may be discrete or continuous, variable or constant value. An example of this function is the use of composite risk index, which is defined as a product of likelihood and consequence value. For each asset, a risk acceptance function specifies how much risk likelihood and consequence is acceptable for that asset. Furthermore, when the user specifies the associated risks along with the likelihood and consequence of each of the risk, the acceptability of risk is based on the pre-defined acceptable risk levels for each asset. Should the risk be acceptable the treatment is not required. However, if the risk is unacceptable, treatment is required to mitigate the risk. Hence, for all the risks to be mitigated, the treatments are required. These treatments serve as requirements for the Cloud services which the user desires. Typical examples of treatments are data location guaranteed in certain geographical region, availability of customer support, guarantees of provider's financial stability etc.

Based on the treatments, the required properties of the Cloud services are identified. The data gathering module in DSS evaluates the Cloud services on the basis of the user identified treatments. The DSS then performs service matchmaking. This process involves providing an aggregate score on the basis of all the treatments chosen by the user and a grading the Cloud services. The closest match to the user requirements forms the most eligible recommendation. In the next section, we provide the technical implementation of these concepts for the development of DSS.

2.7 Technical Challenges and Implementation

Overview of Technology Supporting DSS

Implementation of the decision support system design within the scope of the MODA-Clouds has been developed taking into consideration future data set needs and with assumption that the data set needs to be easily exportable and adaptable to the ever changing nature of the domain which it is exploring. Taking that into account, the core of the data storage is modeled around the graph capable open source database called ArangoDB.[2] ArangoDB is a distributed free and open-source database with flexible data model for documents, graphs, and key-values. For the DSS, documents and graph capabilities of the database are most frequently used. The user interface is developed as a single page web application in JavaScript with technologies like AngularJS, used for all the user interactions and user feedback mechanisms and NodeJS which used for xml validation against xsd plus additional end points to automate the collection of data from other parts of the project. DSS main automatic data collection modules are designed as a standalone tools written in Scala programming language. All the modules developed for the data collection can be easily extended or embedded as libraries in the existing application to be adapted to the specific data gathering process needs.

User Data Gathering Implementation

A set of coherent UI elements have been used, including standard and enhanced selections mechanisms. This will gather the requirements in an organized, comprehensible fashion and accommodate the fact that the selection requirements are incremental sets specified by the multiple actors.

The primary selection tool is a searchable single selection list box. The list is populated based on the previous steps or the internally specified connections. The select menu is presented across all the selection steps. Other techniques such as a slider represent the data type with predefined ranges, at times with legend. The slider allows the user to see all the ranges at once and gives direct visual feedback on scale construction.

The process by itself is constructed as a six step wizard that allows the user to see the current context across the full selection.

Cloud Services Data Gathering Implementation

The automatic data gathering process of the decision support tool is composed of two main modules; data import and data save. Those modules are design to work as a part of the application as well as the standalone modules. The data import module is responsible for the data extraction and data transformation from the structured data sources. The module is able to consume the structured data from the flat file local data sauces in JSON, XML and XLSX formats and respective over the network representations of such structures, like REST, ODATA and WSDL http end points. The output of this module is JSON, which can be invoke as an input for the data saved

---

[2]https://www.arangodb.com//.

module. The data save module is designed to consume predefined modeled JSON input in order to represent and build graph based data structures used by the process service match making based on the user specified requirements. This module is able to build up or enrich the data set based on the data specification.

- **Sharing Process**: In order to enable optimal requirement selection, the DSS allows multiple actors to participate during the definition of the set of requirements the service needs to provide. This approach for data gathering ensured the development of the selection sharing process. This allows an actor to save the current set of selected assets, risks and treatments along with the selected values and representation selection. The export file allows the user to share the fulfilled selection with other actors using preferred sharing medium. Multiple sets of predefined selections can be saved and shared to more closely target parts of the process to the appropriate actor.
- **Visualization**: The Decision Support system has been equipped with multiple data visualizations in order to simplify the overview and understanding of the user process, the mechanisms of understanding the selection criteria interaction and data connections.
- **Multi-Cloud specific features**: The DSS also supports the mitigation of risks particular to the multi-Cloud environment by assessing the risks related to selection of a group of services. For example the DSS warns users in the case of a vendor lock-in in a selection of services by evaluating the providers for all the services in the selection. The DSS also provides an evaluation of ease of migration out of any service by assessing the different dimensions that support migration capabilities in a service. These properties provide a holistic vision of the solution matched to a Multi-cloud environment.

2.8 Conclusion: Evolution of Cloud Services, Decision Support and Future Work

This chapter discusses the use of a decision support system to simplify the choice of services that match functional and non-functional requirements. This DSS uniquely uses risk management techniques to compliment the requirements used to deliver a qualified list of services for composition. Some of the decision criteria are subjective and the use of decision support to simplify choices removes the need for service choices based on multi-factor optimised expert systems. Cloud services evolving into a wider architectural movement that includes containers and microservices. Cloud services used in a multi-cloud environment linked with microservices and container API are leading to a multi-service style of architecture, building applications based on component oriented development. This is more suitable to agile and DevOps development mapping services to agile user stories and components. The number of internal and external services available for developers is already increasing and there will be a need to identify, classify and describe services in a common way to remove redundancy and improve development times. This evolution is increasingly demanding service description, discovery and matchmaking capabilities that can benefit from decision support of the type described in this chapter. Data gathering remains a legally and technically difficult area, potentially preventing all but the most simplistic of services choices being made. This is an area of future investigation, possibly in collaboration with some of the cloud standardisation initiatives and organisations such as the Cloud Security Alliance and Cloud Industry Forum.

Reference

1. Siegel J, Perdue J (2012) Cloud services measures for global use: the service measurement index (SMI). In: 2012 Annual SRRI global conference. Carnegie Mellon University, Silicon Valley, Mountain View, CA, USA

Chapter 3
The MODAClouds Model-Driven Development

Nicolas Ferry, Marcos Almeida and Arnor Solberg

3.1 Introduction

The Cloud computing market encompasses an ever-growing number of providers offering a multitude of infrastructure-as-a-service (IaaS) and platform-as-a-service (PaaS) solutions. In order to exploit the peculiarities of each Cloud solution as well as to optimize performances, availability, and cost, an emergent need is to run and manage multi-Cloud applications [1] (i.e., applications that can execute on multiple Cloud infrastructures and platforms). However, current stacks, libraries and frameworks lack in software engineering methodologies and tools to design, deploy and maintain multi-Cloud systems as stated in the CORDIS reports on Cloud computing [2, 3], "*whilst a distributed data environment (IaaS) cannot be easily moved to any platform provider (PaaS) […], it is also almost impossible to move a service/image/environment between providers on the same level.*"

Model-Driven Development (MDD) [4] techniques are particularly useful to address these challenges. They allow shifting the paradigm from code-centric to model-centric. Models are thus the main artefacts of the development process and enable developers to work at a high level of abstraction, focusing on Cloud concerns rather than implementation details. Model transformations help automating the work of going from abstract concepts to implementation. This approach, which is commonly summarized as "*model once, generate anywhere*", is thus particularly relevant when it comes to design and management of applications across multiple Clouds,

N. Ferry · A. Solberg (✉)
Stiftelsen SINTEF, Postbox 4760 Sluppen, 7465 Trondheim, Norway
e-mail: arnor.solberg@sintef.no

N. Ferry
e-mail: nicolas.ferry@sintef.no

M. Almeida
Softeam Cadextan, 21 Avenue Victor Hugo, 75016 Paris, France
e-mail: marcos.almeida@softeam.fr

E. Di Nitto et al. (eds.), *Model-Driven Development and Operation of Multi-Cloud Applications*, PoliMI SpringerBriefs,
DOI 10.1007/978-3-319-46031-4_3

as well as migrating them from one Cloud to another. Moreover, models can also be used to reason about the application Quality of Service (QoS), and to support design-time exploration methods that identify the Cloud deployment configuration of minimum cost, while satisfying QoS constraints.

In this chapter we present the MODAClouds Model-Driven Development approach to support the design of multi-Cloud applications with guaranteed QoS. The proposed approach relies on a set of tool-supported domain-specific languages (DSLs) collectively called MODACloudML. MODACloudML enables managing multi-Cloud applications in a Cloud provider-independent way while still exploiting the peculiarities of each IaaS and PaaS solution. By supporting both IaaS and PaaS, MODACloudML enables several levels of control of multi-Cloud applications by the Models@runtime engine (see Chap. 9): (i) in case of executing on IaaS or white box PaaS solutions; full control with automatic provisioning and deployment of the entire Cloud stack from the infrastructure to the application, or (ii) in case of executing on black box PaaS solutions; partial control of the application (note that if parts of the multi-Cloud application executes on IaaS or white box PaaS, MODACloudML provides full control of those parts).

The remainder of this chapter is organized as follows. Section 3.2 overviews the typical design process using the MODAClouds design-time tools and MODACloudML. Section 3.3 presents the overall architecture of MODACloudML. Section 3.4 details the list of models that compose MODACloudML before providing examples of some of them. Finally Sect. 3.5 presents some related works and Sect. 3.6 draws some conclusions.

3.2 The Design-Time Development Process

MODACloudML targets different profiles of users, from application developers and providers, who are concerned about the actual deployment artifacts and scripts, to QoS engineers, concerned with application performance and architectural costs. In order to support such diverse profiles, the MODAClouds Integrated Development Environment provides automation tools that facilitate the transition between different models by means of model-to-model transformations. It also provides model-to-text transformations that allow the developer to export/import models from/to specialized tools such as the QoS modelling and analysis tools from MODAClouds.

Designing a Cloud application through the design-time environment is typically a multi-stage process as depicted in Fig. 3.1. First, users specify, through the IDE, the application architecture and all its functional aspects as well as QoS requirements. In the next stage, designers may decide to refine these models, for instance, by selecting a certain class of database services and certain kinds of computational resources. In MODAClouds, this process is achieved by QoS engineers supported by the Line and SPACE 4Clouds tools (see Chap. 4). Line can be used to estimate the performance of the identified solution (e.g., response time and throughput), whilst SPACE 4Clouds can be used to find the minimum-cost multi-Cloud deployment configuration. At this

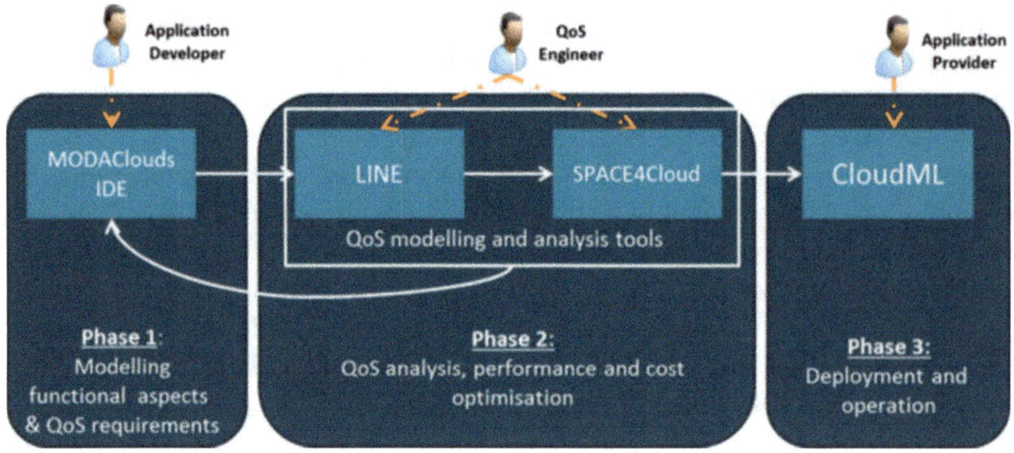

Fig. 3.1 MODAClouds design-time approach workflow

stage, an iterative process may be started to tune the models of the application until a suitable solution is identified. The output of this process is a CLOUDML deployment model that can then be used by the application provider to automatically deploy the multi-Cloud application.

All these tools rely and can be used to produce the models that compose MODA-CloudML. In the next sections we present the overall architecture of MODAClouds as well as the list of models it is made of.

3.3 Overall Language Architecture

The MODACloudML architecture is inspired by the OMG Model-Driven Architecture (MDA) [5], which is a model-based approach for the development of software systems. The MDA relies on three types of models for three layers of abstractions. The closer to the system a layer is, the more technical the description. These three MDA layers, from the more abstract to the more detailed, are:

- The Computational Independent Model (CIM), which describes what the system is expected to do but hides all the technical details related to the implementation of the system.
- The Platform Independent Model (PIM), which describes views of the systems in a platform independent manner so that it can be mapped to several platforms at the PSM levels.
- The Platform Specific Model (PSM), which refines the PIM with technical details required for specifying how the system can use a specific platform.

Some of the main benefits of the MDA are to facilitate the portability, interoperability and reusability of parts of the system which can be easily moved from one platform to another, as well as the maintenance of the system through human readable and reusable specifications at various levels of abstraction.

From the Cloud perspective, the introduction of new layers of abstraction improves the portability and reusability of Cloud related concerns amongst several Clouds. Indeed, even if the system is designed for a specific platform including framework, middleware, or Cloud services, these entities often rely on similar concepts, which can be abstracted from the specificities of each Cloud provider. Typically, the topology of the system in the Cloud as well as the minimum hardware resources required to run it (e.g., CPU, RAM) can be defined in a Cloud-agnostic way. Thanks to this new abstraction layer, one can map a platform specific model to one or more Cloud providers.

The MODACloudML architecture refines the PSM abstraction layer by dividing it into two sub-levels: the Cloud Provider-Independent Models (CPIM) level and the Cloud Provider-Specific Models (CPSM) level, whilst the CIM and PIM can be grouped into a so called Cloud-enabled Computational Independent Model (CCIM) level. MODACloudML thus relies on the following three layers of abstraction: (i) the Cloud-enabled Computation Independent Model to describe an application and its data, (ii) the Cloud-Provider Independent Model to describe Cloud concerns related to the application in a Cloud-agnostic way, and (iii) the Cloud-Provider Specific Model to describe the Cloud concerns needed to deploy and provision the application on a specific Cloud.

3.4 MODACloudML Sub Models

The models that compose MODACLoudML are presented and organised according to the modelling level they belong in Fig. 3.2.

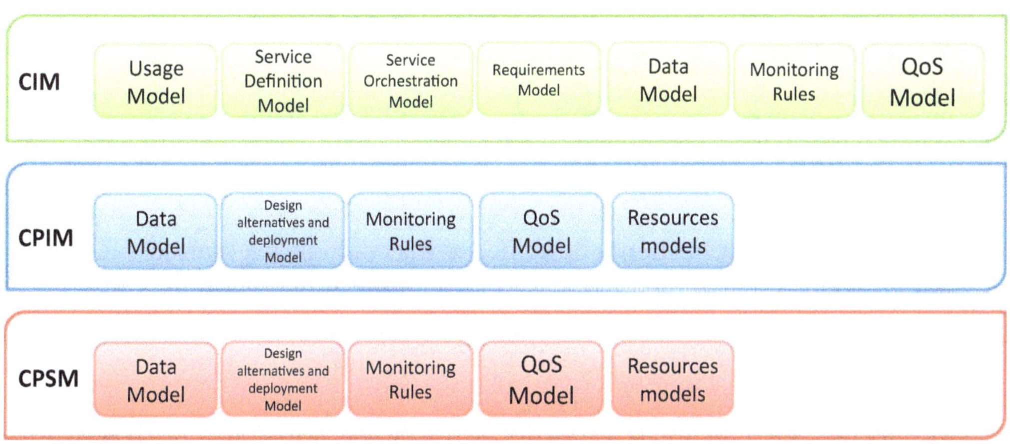

Fig. 3.2 The MODACloudML models

3.4.1 CCIM Models

The CCIM models, which define what the system is expected to do but hide the Cloud-related concerns, are the following:

Service Definition Model: describes the software to be developed as a set of components or services. It includes the typical constructs needed for describing the structure of a software system.

Usage Model: specifies the way users are expected to exploit the functionality of the software to be. It consider a 24 h time-horizon. Each single point in time of the usage model can be exploited by QoS tools regarding the search for optimal solutions.

Service Orchestration: describes the behaviour of the glue between components and services. It can be annotated with stochastic information used to express the probability for some behavioural path to be followed which can in turn be exploited by QoS analysis and optimisation tools.

Requirements Model: completes and formalizes the service functional description. Business and QoS requirements can be associated to a Service or to a specific service operation.

Data Model: describes the main data structures associated with the software to be. It can be expressed in terms of typical Entity Relational (ER) diagrams and enriched by a metamodel that specifies functional and non-functional data properties.

QoS Model: includes information concerning expected QoS characteristics (e.g., response time) at the application level. QoS contraints can be attached to specific application component/services.

In the following we exemplify the usage of the Service Orchestration models to specify the overall architecture of the SensApp case study.

3.4.2 Example

At the CCIM level, an application is described as a set of high level services following a Service Oriented Architecture (SOA) [6]. The application is specified as a set of business-aligned reusable services that can be combined into high-level business processes and solutions within the context of an enterprise.

Figure 3.3 depicts a simple functional architecture of the SensApp case study specified with the MODAClouds IDE as a Service Orchestration model. SensApp [7] is a typical Cloud-based application that acts as a buffer between sensor networks and Cloud-based systems. On the one hand, it facilitates sensors to continuously push data while, on the other hand, it provides higher level services with notification and query facilities.

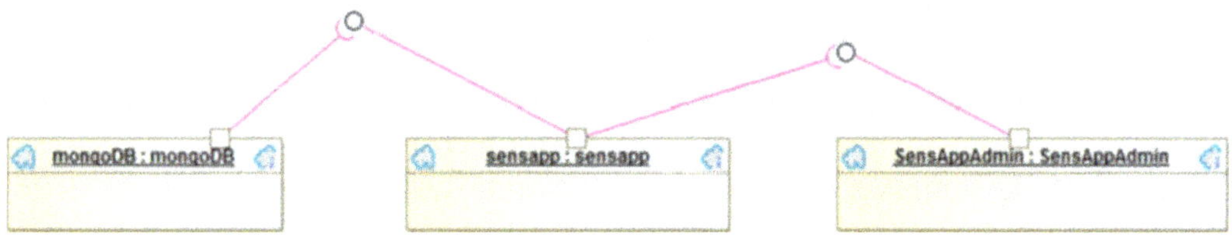

Fig. 3.3 SensApp CCIM architecture

The overall architecture of SensApp consists of a core service called *SensApp* to manage the sensors and their data coupled with a MongoDB[1] database to store sensor descriptions and meta-data as well as the measurements. The *SensApp admin* uses the public REST API of *SensApp* and provides capabilities to manage sensors and visualise data using a graphical user interface. For the sake of simplicity, other concerns such as the detailed description of interfaces, or the behaviour of services and users are not presented in this figure.

The models at the CCIM level are used to semi-automatically generate part of the CPIM models. In particular, the Service Definition Models and the Service Orchestrations Model, which can partially be generated through reverse engineering techniques, are used to initiate the Design Alternatives and deployment models whilst the CCIM data models are used to initiate the CPIM data models.

3.4.3 *CPIM and CPSM Models*

CPIM and CPSM levels are composed of the same set of models. CPIM models are derived from CCIM models and are in turn refined into CPSM models. The set of models that compose these two levels are the following:

Design Alternative and Deployment Model: at the CPIM level, it describes the assignment of application components to underlying resources. This includes services, platforms and infrastructural resources. At the CPSM level, it characterizes Cloud resources of a specific Cloud provider.

Data Model: at the CPIM level, this model refines the CCIM data model to describe data model in terms of logical models as flat model, hierarchical model and relational model. Finally, at the CPSM level, it describes the data model based on the specific data structures implemented by the Cloud providers.

Monitoring Rules: this model describes the monitoring rules aiming at controlling the execution of specific application components/data/connectors assigned to specific resources. They are used to indicate to the run-time platform what components/services to monitor.

[1] https://www.mongodb.org.

QoS Model: this model includes information concerning QoS characteristics of Cloud resources in both a provider-independent (CPIM level) and provider-specific (CPSM level) way. It includes cost information, thus, offering the possibility to estimate an upper-bound for application costs.

Resources Model: this model represents different Cloud environment and offerings and can be used as a catalogue of available resources. This catalogue is particularly useful as a basis for the specification of CPIM and CPSM models. It is also used in order to evaluate performance and cost of applications, as proposed by the decision making and analysis tools, as well as during the selection of the resource to be used by a multi-Cloud application.

In the following we exemplify the usage of the deployment model to specify the component deployment and orchestration in the Cloud. Deployment models are specified using CLOUDML.

CLOUDML [8, 9] consists of: (i) a domain-specific language (DSL) for specifying the provisioning and deployment of multi-Cloud applications; and (ii) a models@runtime environment for enacting the provisioning, deployment, and adaptation of these applications. While the CLOUDML language is part of MODACloudML, the models@runtime environment is integrated as part of the MODAClouds IDE. This way, developers can take advantage of the CCIM models and of the optimization tools in order to specify deployment models. CLOUDML allows developers to model the provisioning and deployment of a multi-Cloud application at both the CPIM and CPSM levels of abstractions. This two-level approach is agnostic to any development paradigm and technology, meaning that the application developers can design and implement their applications based on their preferred paradigms and technologies.

CLOUDML is inspired by component-based approaches [10] that facilitate separation of concerns and reusability. In this respect, deployment models can be regarded as assemblies of components exposing ports (or interfaces), and bindings between these ports. In a nutshell, CLOUDML enables to express the following concepts (we refer the reader to [9] for details):

- **Cloud**: Represents a collection of VMs offered by a particular Cloud provider.
- **External component**: Represents a reusable type of VM or PaaS solution.
- **Internal component**: Represents a reusable type of application component to be deployed on an external component.
- **Port**: Represents a required or provided interface to a feature of a component.
- **Relationship**: Represents a communication between ports of two application components, they express dependencies between components.
- **Hosting**: Represents the fact that a component uses another as execution platform.

In addition, CLOUDML implements the type-instance pattern [11], which also facilitates reusability. This pattern exploits two flavors of typing, namely ontological and linguistic [12]. Figure 3.4 illustrates these two flavors of typing. SL (for Small Linux) represents a reusable type of VM. It is linguistically typed by the class VM (for Virtual Machine). SL1 represents an instance of the VM SL. It is ontologically typed by SL and linguistically typed by VMInstance.

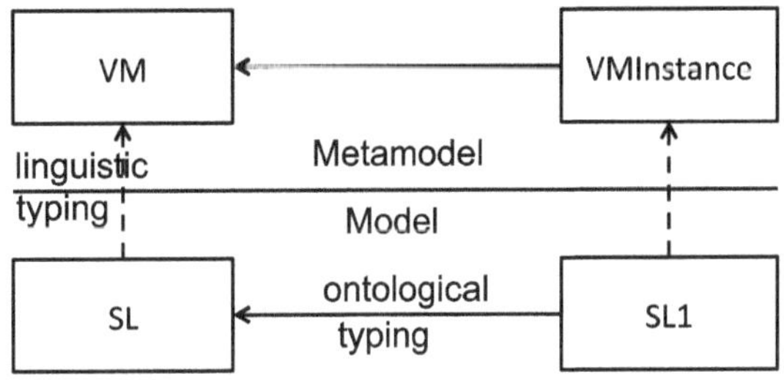

Fig. 3.4 Linguistic and ontological typing

The transformation from CPIM to CPSM consists in: (i) adding the actual data resulting from the resolution of the constraints defined in the external component types (e.g., actual number of cores, RAM size, storage size), and (ii) adding data required for the deployment and management of the application that are Cloud provider-specific. Thanks to this enrichment, it is possible to retrieve data about the actual resources provisioned including how they can be accessed and how they can be configured. Such data is particularly useful during the process of configuration of the components and their bindings.

3.4.4 Example

Figure 3.5 depicts the deployment model of SensApp at the CPIM level specified with the MODAClouds IDE. The overall system will be deployed using two different virtual machines (VMs), the first VM will host SensApp and the second the SensApp Admin. Both VMs (*CloudNodeInstance* and *ML*) have differents characteristics and are thus specified as instances of different types (*SL* and *ML*). Both SensApp and its admin, in order to be executed properly, have to be hosted in a Servlet container. In this case they are both hosted on the same type of Jetty container called *JettySC*. This type of relationship is depicted in the figure by arrows between blue ports. In addition, SensApp has to communicate with the database in order to store and retrieve sensors data. This type of relationship is depicted by arrows between purple ports.

3.5 Related Work

In the literature several efforts aimed to offer support for designing, optimizing and managing multi-Cloud applications. In particular, several EU projects provide methodologies and tools to support the design and management of Cloud-based applications. However, to the best of our knowledge, none of them propose an integrated approach offering models that can be used for performance and cost analysis and optimisation, as well as deployment and runtime management of multi-Cloud applications.

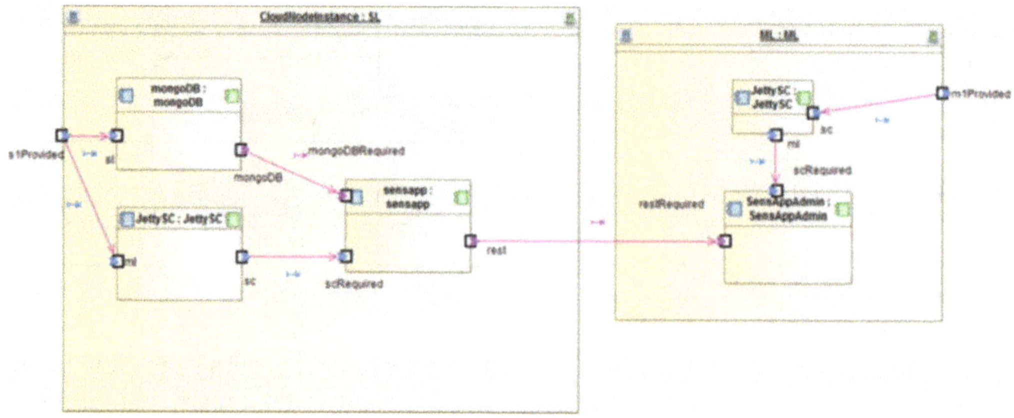

Fig. 3.5 Deployment model of SensApp at the CPIM level

The Cloud Application Modeling Language (CAML) [13] is being developed within the ARTIST EU FP7 project[2] and supports the provider-independent specification of deployment topologies and their refinement into provider-specific deployment. The main focus of the ARTIST project being the migration of legacy application to the Cloud as well as the feasibility study of such migration, the language has been defined as an UML internal modeling language based on a model library and profiles. This way, it can be directly applied on UML models, which is especially beneficial for migration scenarios where reverse-engineered UML models are tailored towards a selected Cloud environment. These CAML profiles also capture Cloud offerings from a functional and non-functional perspectives including cost aspects.

In order to cover the necessary aspects of the specification and execution of multi-Cloud applications, the PaaSage project[3] adopts the Cloud Application Modelling and Execution Language (CAMEL). CAMEL integrates and extends existing DSLs, including Cloud Modelling Language (CLOUDML) [8, 9], Saloon [14, 15], and the Organisation part of CERIF [16], for specifying multiple aspects of multi-Cloud applications, such as provisioning, deployment, providers, organisations, users, and roles. Moreover, CAMEL adds DSLs for specifying aspects such as metrics, requirements, goals, scalability rules [17, 18], security controls, execution contexts, execution histories, etc. CAMEL is designed and implemented with the Eclipse Modelling Framework (EMF)[4] on top of the Connected Data Objects (CDO)[5] persistence solution. MODAClouds and PaaSage are collaborating on the research and development of CLOUDML. However, PaaSage does not offer a specific approach for the design-time optimization of multi-Cloud applications.

The Topology and Orchestration Specification for Cloud Applications (TOSCA) [19, 20] is a specification developed by the OASIS consortium, which provides a

[2]http://www.artist-project.eu/.

[3]https://www.paasage.eu.

[4]https://www.eclipse.org/modeling/emf/.

[5]https://www.eclipse.org/cdo/.

language for specifying the components comprising the topology of Cloud-based applications along with the processes for their orchestration. TOSCA is comparable to CLOUDML, however the language has been conceived for design-time modelling only.

3.6 Conclusion

The MODAClouds Model-Driven Development approach relies on the so called MODACloudML which integrates a set of domain-specific languages. These languages cover the specifications of both functional and non functional aspects of multi-Cloud applications. Thanks to the three levels architecture, multi-Cloud applications can be designed in a Cloud provider-independent way thus reducing vendor lock-in before being refined with provider-specific information thus allowing to exploit the peculiarities of each provider.

References

1. Petcu D (2014) Consuming resources and services from multiple clouds. J Grid Comput 1–25
2. SSAI Expert Group (2010) The future of cloud computing. Technical report
3. SSAI Expert Group (2012) A roadmap for advanced cloud technologies under H2020. Technical report
4. Schmidt DC (2006) Guest editor's introduction: model-driven engineering. IEEE Comput 39(2):25–31
5. OMG: OMG model-driven architecture. http://www.omg.org/mda/
6. MacKenzie M, Laskey K, McCabe F, Brown P, Metz R (2006) Reference model for service oriented architecture 1.0. Technical report, OASIS
7. Mosser S, Fleurey F, Morin B, Chauvel F, Solberg A, Goutier I (2012) SENSAPP as a reference platform to support cloud experiments: from the internet of things to the internet of services. In: SYNASC 2012: 14th international symposium on symbolic and numeric algorithms for scientific computing. IEEE Computer Society, pp 400–406
8. Ferry N, Rossini A, Chauvel F, Morin B, Solberg A (2013) Towards model-driven provisioning, deployment, monitoring, and adaptation of multi-cloud systems. In: O'Conner L (ed) Proceedings of CLOUD 2013: 6th IEEE international conference on cloud computing. IEEE Computer Society, pp 887–894
9. Ferry N, Song H, Rossini A, Chauvel F, Solberg A (2014) CloudMF: applying MDE to tame the complexity of managing multi-cloud applications. In: Proceedings of UCC 2014: 7th IEEE/ACM international conference on utility and cloud computing
10. Szyperski C (2011) Component software: beyond object-oriented programming, 2nd edn. Addison-Wesley Professional
11. Atkinson C, Kühne T (2002) Rearchitecting the UML infrastructure. ACM Trans Model Comput Simul 12(4):290–321
12. Kühne T (2006) Matters of (meta-)modeling. Softw Syst Model 5(4):369–385
13. Bergmayr A, Troya J, Neubauer P, Wimmer M, Kappel G (2014) UML-based cloud application modeling with libraries, profiles and templates. In: Proceedings of workshop on CloudMDE, pp 56–65

14. Quinton C, Rouvoy R, Duchien L (2012) Leveraging feature models to configure virtual appliances. In: CloudCP 2012: 2nd international workshop on cloud computing platforms. ACM, pp 2:1–2:6
15. Quinton C, Haderer N, Rouvoy R, Duchien L (2013) Towards multi-cloud configurations using feature models and ontologies. In: MultiCloud 2013: international workshop on multi-cloud applications and federated clouds. ACM, pp 21–26
16. Jeffery K, Houssos N, Jörg B, Asserson A (2014) Research information management: the CERIF approach. IJMSO 9(1):5–14
17. Kritikos K, Domaschka J, Rossini A ((2014 (To Appear))) SRL: a scalability rule language for multi-cloud environments. In: Proceedings of CloudCom 2014: 6th IEEE international conference on cloud computing technology and science
18. Domaschka J, Kritikos K, Rossini A ((2014 (To Appear))) Towards a generic language for scalability rules. In: Proceedings of CSB 2014: 2nd international workshop on cloud service brokerage
19. Palma D, Spatzier T (2013) Topology and orchestration specification for cloud applications (TOSCA). Technical report, Organization for the Advancement of Structured Information Standards (OASIS) (June)
20. Kopp O, Binz T, Breitenbücher U, Leymann F (2013) Winery–a modeling tool for tosca-based cloud applications. In: Service-oriented computing. Springer, pp 700–704

Chapter 4
QoS Assessment and SLA Management

Danilo Ardagna, Michele Ciavotta, Giovanni Paolo Gibilisco, Riccardo Benito Desantis, Giuliano Casale, Juan F Pérez, Francesco D'Andria and Román Sosa González

4.1 Introduction

Verifying that a software system shows certain non-functional properties is a primary concern for Cloud applications.[1] Given the heterogeneous technology offer and the related pricing models currently available in the Cloud market it is extremely complex to find the deployment that fits the application requirements, and provides the best Quality of Service (QoS) and cost trade-offs. This task can be very

[1]In this chapter non-functional properties, QoS and non-functional requirements will be used interchangeably.

D. Ardagna (✉) · M. Ciavotta · G.P. Gibilisco · R.B. Desantis
DEIB, Politecnico di Milano, Piazza L. da Vinci, 32, 20133 Milano, Italy
e-mail: danilo.ardagna@polimi.it

M. Ciavotta
e-mail: michele.ciavotta@polimi.it

G.P. Gibilisco
e-mail: giovannipaolo.gibilisco@polimi.it

R.B. Desantis
e-mail: riccardobenito.desantis@polimi.it

G. Casale · J.F. Pérez
Department of Computing, Imperial College, 180 Queens Gate, London SW7 2AZ, UK
e-mail: g.casale@imperial.ac.uk

J.F. Pérez
e-mail: j.perez-bernal@imperial.ac.uk

F. D'Andria · R. Sosa González
ATOS Spain SA, Subida al Mayorazgo 24B Planta 1, 38110 Santa Cruz de Tenerife, Spain
e-mail: francesco.dandria@atos.net

R. Sosa González
e-mail: roman.sosa@atos.net

E. Di Nitto et al. (eds.), *Model-Driven Development and Operation of Multi-Cloud Applications*, PoliMI SpringerBriefs,
DOI 10.1007/978-3-319-46031-4_4

challenging, even infeasible if performed manually, since the number of solutions may become extremely large depending on the number of possible providers and available technology stacks. Furthermore, Cloud systems are inherently multi-tenant and their performance can vary with the time of day, depending on the congestion level, policies implemented by the Cloud provider, and the competition among running applications.

MODAClouds envisions design abstractions that help the QoS Engineer to specify non-functional requirements and tools to evaluate and compare multiple Cloud architectures, evaluating cost and performance considering the distinctive traits of the Cloud.

To better understand the scope of the MODAClouds QoS and SLA tools, referred to as **SPACE 4Clouds for Dev—QoS Modelling and Analysis tool**, Fig. 4.1 provides a high-level overview of the architecture and main actors involved. Each of these tools is the topic of the upcoming sections. In Figure we depict how the Feasibility Study engineer, the Application Developer and the QoS engineer provide inputs to this MODAClouds module. The Feasibility Study engineer provides a set of candidate providers for the application under development. The application developer instead creates a consistent application model and a set of architectural constraints using MODACloudML meta-models (see Chap. 3). Ultimately, the QoS engineer is in charge to define suitable QoS constraints. Simply put, the tool receives in input a set of models describing an application both in terms of functionalities and resource demands. At this point two possible scenarios are possible, in the first one the QoS engineer uses the tool in assessment mode, namely she evaluates the performance and cost based on a specific application deployment (which includes type and number of VMs and PaaS services). In the second scenario the QoS engineer provides

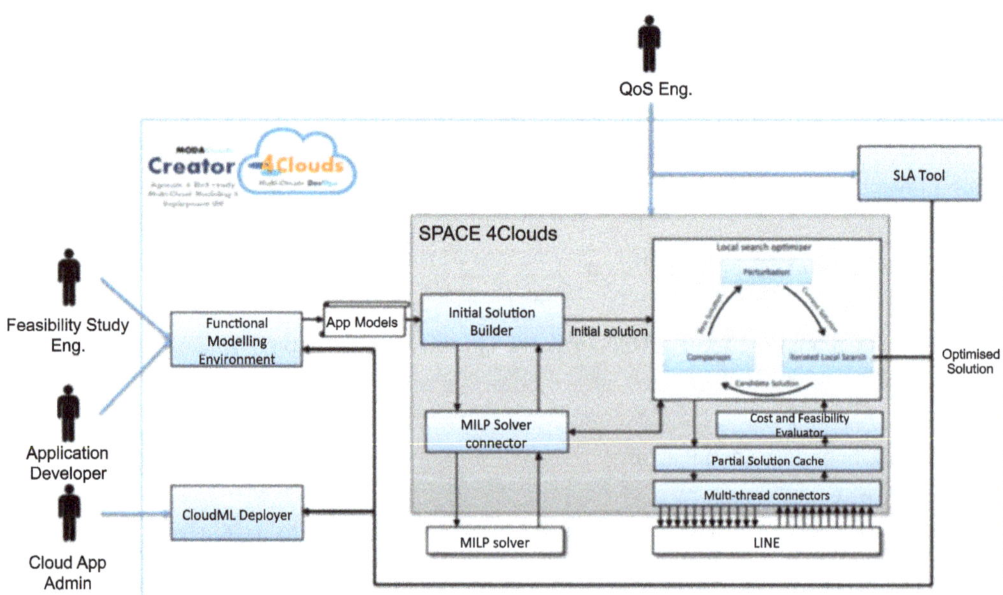

Fig. 4.1 SPACE 4Clouds for Dev—high-level architecture

only a partial configuration and lets the tool face the task of analysing the possible alternatives to return a cost optimised solution that meets the constraints.

In this latter scenario, the module returns a complete deployment description (set of providers, type of VM per tier, number of VMs per hour, type of other services), and also reports useful information about the overall cost and performance. The QoS engineer at that point may choose to accept the solution as it is, to modify the constraints or to change the deployment and evaluate/force different configurations.

This MODAClouds module is composed of three main components:

- **SPACE 4Clouds** has a twofold function. First, it keeps track of candidate solutions and manages their creation, modification, evaluation, comparison and feasibility check. Second, SPACE 4Clouds deals with the design-space exploration and optimisation process by means of a metaheuristic local-search-based approach.
- **LINE** is the component in charge of the evaluation of the performance models (Layered Queuing Networks—LQN) enriched with information about the efficiency and the dynamic behaviour that can affect the Cloud platform.
- **SLA tool** is the component responsible for generating a formal document describing a Service Level Agreement (SLA) among the involved parties in MODAClouds: customers, application providers and cloud providers.

The rest of this chapter is organised as follows: in Sect. 4.2 the MiC case study is presented, SPACE 4Clouds and LINE are described in Sect. 4.3 whereas the SLA tool is detailed in Sect. 4.4.

4.2 Case Study: Meeting in the Cloud (MiC)

In this section, we introduce a web application called Meeting in the Cloud (MiC) that will be used throughout this chapter as a case study. MiC is a web application for social networking that lets the user to profile her topics of interest and to share them with similar users. Moreover, MiC identifies the most similar users in the network according to the registered users' preferences. More specifically, during the registration process, the new user selects her topics of interest from a set of alternatives, providing a preference for each of them in the range 1–5. At the end of the registration, MiC calculates the Pearson coefficient [1] based on the preferences expressed, identifies the users in the system with the most similar interests, and creates a list of contacts for the newcomer. After the registration process, the user can log in into the MiC portal and interact with her *Best Contacts* by writing and reading posts on the selected topics. Users can also change their interests refining their profiles; in this case the system reacts re-evaluating the similarity and updating the list of recommended contacts.

The application, whose main elements are depicted in Fig. 4.2, comprises a Frontend to process the incoming http requests and a Backend developed using JSP and Servlet technologies. A task queue [2, 3] is used to decouple Frontend and Backend

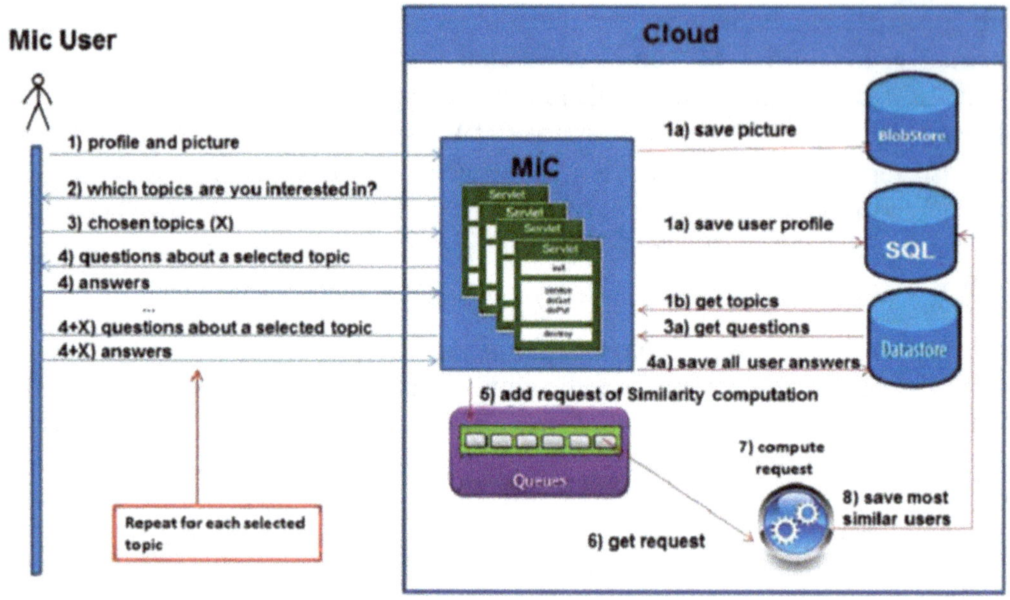

Fig. 4.2 MiC registration steps

in order to make the system capable to evaluate the similarity value in an asynchronous, non-blocking way. The overall application results in this way reactive and responsive all the time. An SQL database stores users' profiles, messages, and best contacts lists. A Blob Service is used to store pictures, while a NoSQL database stores users' interests and preferences. Both are accessed directly by the Frontend. Finally, a Memcache system is used to temporarily store the last retrieved profiles and best contacts messages with the aim of improving the response time of the whole application.

MiC is especially designed to exploit multi Cloud capabilities using a particular Java library, called CPIM, which basically provides an abstraction from the PaaS services provided by the main Cloud Providers, for more details please refer to [4].

4.3 QoS Assessment and Optimisation

SPACE 4Clouds (System PerformAnce and Cost Evaluation on Cloud) is a multi-platform open source tool for the specification, assessment and optimisation of QoS characteristics for Cloud applications. It allows users to describe a software architecture by means of MODACloudML meta-models that express Cloud-specific attributes. Among other things, such models include a user-defined workload in order to assess both performance and cost of the application under different runtime conditions. Users can specify the models defining the Cloud application using Creator 4Clouds graphical interface, while information about the performance of the considered Cloud resources is kept in a SQL database to decouple its evolution from

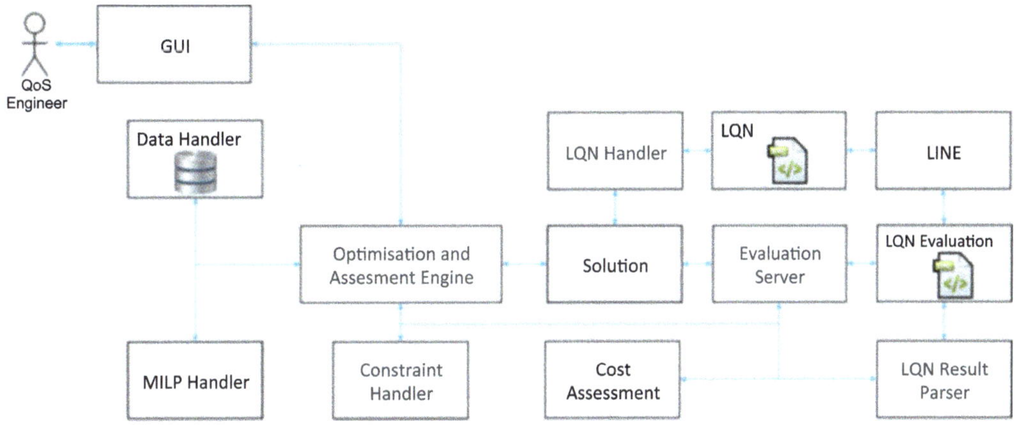

Fig. 4.3 SPACE 4Clouds—architecture

the one of the tool. SPACE 4Clouds can be used either to assess the cost of a complete described solution (i.e. application and Cloud configuration) according to the cost model defined in [5] or (providing only the application model) to find a suitable (even multi-Cloud) configuration that minimises the running cost while meeting QoS requirements.

Figure 4.3 shows the internal structure of SPACE 4Clouds and the main components are:

- *GUI*: consists of a main configuration window that allows loading the application models to be analysed and configuration parameters for the analysis/optimisation process. The GUI also provides some frames used to visualise the results of the assessment and the progress of the optimisation;
- *Solution*: represents the set of classes that form the internal representation of the application. Since a 24 h horizon is considered, the solution stores 24 records with information about configuration, performance, cost and constraint violations.
- *LQN Handler*: maps the internal representation of a solution on the LQN models used by the solver LINE (see Sect. 4.3.3) for the evaluation; the transformation process supports both IaaS and PaaS services and for multi-Cloud deployments. This component is also responsible for the serialisation of the solution in this format before the evaluation and the parsing of the output of LINE.
- *Evaluation Server*: the role of this component is to decouple the evolution of the different phases of the evaluation between the 24 h model instances for each considered provider contained in each solution. This decoupling allows the solution evaluation to happen in parallel.
- *Data Handler*: is the interface between the SQL database and other components of the tool.
- *Cost Assessment*: is the component responsible for the cost evaluation of the solution.
- *Constraint Handler*: is the component responsible to assess the feasibility of the solution with respect to Architectural and QoS constraints. Constraints are defined via a Domain-Specific Language (DSL) for flexibility and extensibility reasons.

- *Optimisation Engine*: It interacts with other components to evaluate the solutions built with respect to cost, feasibility and performance, and it is responsible for finding the optimal deployment configuration. Its core implements a metaheuristic strategy based on a two-level local search with multiple neighbourhoods.

In the following the describe separately the assessment and optimisation scenarios with the help the MiC use case.

4.3.1 Assessment

In this section we consider the assessment scenario, the one in which the QoS engineer uses SPACE 4Clouds to evaluate the cost and performance of the application under development:

1. Through the GUI the QoS engineer loads the models exported by Creator 4Clouds including also a full deployment configuration (list of providers, type and number of VMs and workload share for each hour), and a description of the incoming workload and QoS constraints.
2. The models are translated into 24 LQN instances. Each instance is tailored to model the application deployment in a particular hour of the day. These instances are then used by the Optimisation and Assessment engine to initialise the structure of a SPACE 4Clouds solution.
3. The set of LQN files is fed into the performance engine, usually LINE, which is in charge of executing the performance analysis.
4. The output of the analysis performed by LINE, stored in an XML file, is read by the LQN Handler and written back in the solution.
5. The solution can then be evaluated in terms of feasibility against user defined constraints by the Constraint Handler component.

We consider the MiC use case presented in Sect. 4.2. For the sake of simplicity only Frontend, Backend and a SQL database are considered, packed together and deployed on a single VM. Let us suppose that all the modelling work has been already done and the QoS engineer has to decide the type and the number of VMs for each hour of the day to be allocated to satisfy a set of constraints. Two candidate Cloud providers have been selected, namely Amazon and Microsoft, based upon the pricing models available on the Internet and on the user's experience. The QoS engineer considers that the daily workload for the application under development will likely follow a bimodal distribution, which he can roughly estimate. She also has to consider the non-functional requirements associated with the ongoing project. In our example the CPU utilisation is imposed to be lower than 80 % and the response time of the *register* functionality to be less than 4 s. Using such information, she devises a preliminary Multi-Cloud configuration (5 medium instances allocated on each provider per hour and 50–50 % workload splitting) and loads it along with the application functional model and the constraint set in SPACE 4Clouds; she chooses

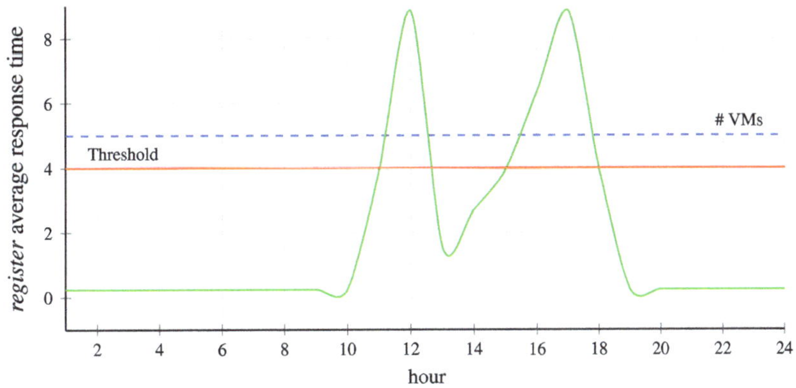

Fig. 4.4 Average response time for MiC *register* functionality

the *assessment* feature and the solution is evaluated and returned. As the reader can see from Fig. 4.4, the response time constraint is violated in the central hours of the day, while the expected daily cost is $34.8.

The solution is clearly infeasible and the QoS engineer has to pull her sleeves up and fine-tune the configuration, perhaps acting on the number of VMs and the workload splitting between the selected Clouds per hour. This is a non-trivial task since, for instance, varying the workload share directed to a certain provider affects the response time and implies an adjustment of the number of VMs running at that particular hour. A similar reasoning applies to the VM types involved. After long fine tuning, the user identifies a feasible solution with the following cost: $39.4. The solution in point has the same types of VMs of the original one and the same workload percentage for each of two providers but uses a larger number of VMs in the hours between 10 a.m. and 19 p.m.

At this point the user can be satisfied with her work but we will see in the next section that there is still room for improvement without sacrificing feasibility, exploiting the optimisation feature of SPACE 4Clouds.

4.3.2 Optimisation

The aim of this section is to provide a brief description of the optimisation strategy implemented within SPACE 4Cloud. A two-step approach has been developed; in the first step an initial valid configuration of the system is derived automatically starting from a partially specified application description given by the QoS engineer. In order to do so, a Mixed Integer Linear Problem (MILP) is built and efficiently solved [6]. This solution is based on approximated performance models, in fact, the QoS associated to a deployment solution is calculated by means of an M/G/1 queuing model with processor sharing policy. Such performance model allows calculating the average response time of a request in closed form. Our goal is to determine quickly an approximated initial solution (list of Cloud providers, types of VMs, number of VMs and hourly load balancing) that is then further improved.

In the second step a local-search-based optimisation algorithm iteratively improves the starting Cloud deployment exploring several configurations. A more expressive performance model (LQN) is employed to derive more accurate estimates of the QoS by means of the LINE solver. More specifically, the algorithm implemented exploits the assessment feature to evaluate several, hopefully distinct Cloud configurations. It has been designed to explore the solution space using a bi-level approach that divides the problem into two levels delegating the assignment of the VM type to the first (upper) level, and the load balancing and the definition of the number of replicas to the second (lower) level. The first level implements a stochastic local search with tabu memory; at each iteration the VM type used for a particular tier is changed randomly from all the available VM types, according to the architectural constraints. The tabu memory is used to store recent moves and avoid cycling of the candidate solutions around the same configurations. Once the VM size is fixed the solution is refined by gradually reducing the number of VMs until the optimal allocation is found. Finally the workload is balanced among the Cloud providers by solving a specific MILP model. This whole process is repeated for a pre-defined number of iterations, updating the final solution each time a feasible and cheaper one is found.

Returning to the example begun in the previous section, let us imagine that the QoS engineer has at her disposal only the functional and non-functional description of the application and an indication on the possible shape and average value of the workload. The user in point can leave to SPACE 4Clouds the task of choosing the most suitable set of providers (limited to two providers for a fair comparison with the scenario in the previous section), the type and number of VMs for each provider and hour, and the hourly workload share for each provider. In this second case a feasible and optimised solution is returned in around 20 min and the related cost is \$19.33 that is 50 % lower than the solution devised by trial and error in the previous section. At this point one may wonder, how is the solution from SPACE 4Clouds different from the one obtained by the QoS engineer? Fig. 4.5 depicts the number of VMs per hour for the selected Cloud providers. We can see that Microsoft has been replaced

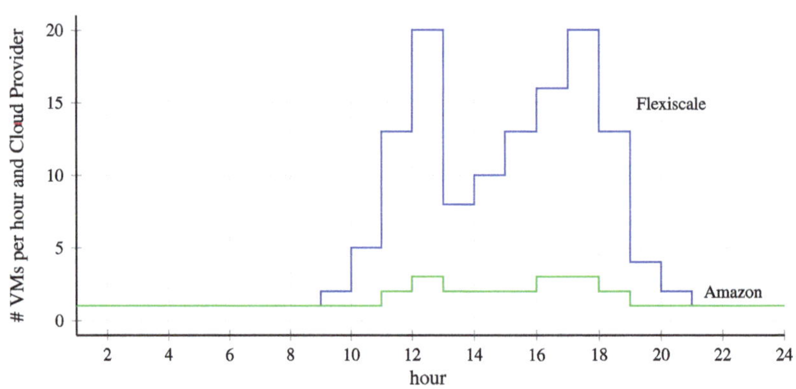

Fig. 4.5 VMs allocated per hour on Amazon and Flexiscale cloud providers

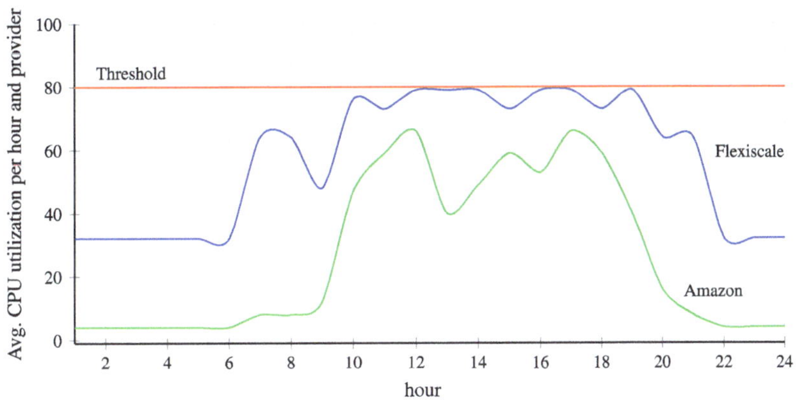

Fig. 4.6 CPU utilization per hour on Amazon and Flexiscale cloud providers

by Flexiscale and that the number of VMs allocated varies hourly from 1 through 20 differently for each provider. Moreover, distinct (more powerful) VM types have been selected and the workload has been split in 80–20 %, where the larger part has been assigned to Flexiscale. Finally, Fig. 4.6 reports the average CPU utilization per Cloud provider, that is clearly below the threshold of 80 % imposed by the user.

4.3.3 LINE

LINE [7] is a tool for the performance analysis of cloud applications. LINE has been designed to automatically build and solve performance models from high-level descriptions of the application. This description can be in the form of a Layered Queueing Network (LQN) model. From this description, LINE is able to provide accurate estimates of relevant performance measures such as application response time or server utilisation. LINE can also provide response times for specific components of the application, enabling the pinpointing of components causing a degradation in the QoS. LINE can therefore be used at design time to diagnose whether the deployment characteristics are adequate to attain the desired QoS levels.

Although other tools are available for performance modelling (such as SimuCom [8] and LQNS [9]), LINE stands apart for a number of reasons.

- In addition to provide average performance measures, LINE can compute *response time distributions*, which can be directly used to assess *percentile Service Level Agreements* (SLAs), e.g., that 95 % of the requests for the *register* functionality are processed in less than 6 s.
- LINE features a reliability model, namely *random environments* [10], to capture a number of conditions that may affect the application, including servers breakdowns and repairs, slow start-up times, resource heterogeneity and contention in multi-tenancy, a key property of cloud deployments.

- LINE is able to model *general request processing times*, which can be used to represent the resource demands posed by the very broad range of cloud applications.
- LINE offers a parallel execution mode for the efficient solution of a large number of performance models.

4.4 SLA Management

As far as SLA management is concerned, in the MODAClouds context we consider three possible actors, Cloud Service Providers (CSPs), which are responsible for the efficient utilization of the physical resources and guarantees their availability for the customers; Application Providers (APs) that are responsible for the efficient utilization of their allocated resources in order to satisfy the SLA established with their customers (end users) and achieve their business goals and customers, which represent the legitimate users for the services offered by the application providers. Usually, CSPs charge APs for renting Cloud resources to host their applications. APs, in turn, may charge their Customers for the use of their services and need to guarantee their customers' SLA. SLA violations, indeed, have an impact on APs reputation and revenue loss incurred in the case of Cloud-hosted business applications. In both circumstances penalty-based policies have to be enforced.

MODAClouds therefore devises a two-level SLA system; the first level (Customer-AP) describes the service offered by the Application Provider to its users. The guarantee terms in this SLA should only watch observable metrics by the end user. At the other level, AP-CP SLA describes the QoS expected from the Cloud provider. In this SLA level, there is one agreement per Virtual Machine or PaaS service.

The lifecycle of an SLA can be split up in several different phases:

1. preparation of the service offer as a **template**,
2. location and mediation of the **agreement**,
3. **assessment** of the agreement during execution and
4. termination and decommission of the agreement.

Within MODAClouds we designed and implemented a policy-driven SLA framework that focus on the phase 1–3 of the described lifecycle. It comprises a REST server (the SLA core) and a set of additional helper tools: the SLA Mediator and the SLA Dashboard. The Mediator tool acts as a layer atop the core, to implement some MODAClouds specific behaviour. The SLA Dashboard shows the violations and penalties of agreements in a more user-friendly way.

Figure 4.7 shows how the SLA Components are organised and how they are related to other MODAClouds components, in particular:

- SLA Repository: manages the persistence of SLA Templates, SLA Contracts and the relation between Services/Contracts/Templates.

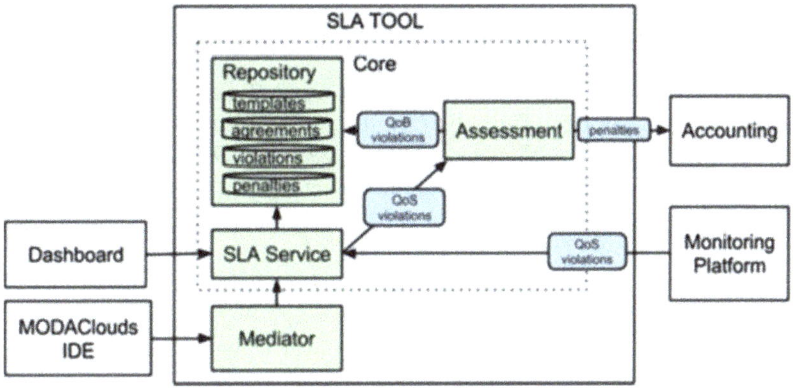

Fig. 4.7 SLA tool: architecture

- SLA Mediator: maps the QoS constraints defined by the QoS Engineer in SLA Agreements of both SLA levels.
- Assessment: computes the possible business violations, notifying any observer (like an external Accounting component) of raised penalties.

Finally, we want to remark that the tool has been implemented following to be fully compliant (concepts, agreements and templates) with the WS-Agreement[2] specification. This choice made it a tool more flexible and potentially applicable to contexts other than MODAClouds.

References

1. Pearson K (1895) Note on regression and inheritance in the case of two parents. Proc R Soc Lond 58:240–242
2. Gamma E, Helm R, Johnson R, Vlissides J (1995) Design patterns: elements of reusable object-oriented software. Addison-Wesley Longman Publishing Co. Inc
3. Schmidt D, Stal M, Rohnert H, Buschmann F (2001) Pattern-oriented software architecture patterns for concurrent and networked objects. Wiley
4. Giove F, Longoni D, Yancheshmeh SM, Ardagna D, Di Nitto E (2013) An approach for the development of portable applications on PaaS clouds. Closer 2013 Proc Aachen Ger 30:591–601
5. Franceschelli D. and Ardagna D. and Ciavotta M. and Di Nitto E.: SPACE4CLOUD: a tool for system performance and costevaluation of cloud systems. Proceedings of the 2013 international workshop on multi-cloud applications and federated clouds, 2013, pp 27–34
6. Ardagna D, Gibilisco GP, Ciavotta M, Lavrentev A (2014) A multi-model optimization framework for the model driven design of cloud applications. Search-Based Softw Eng 8636:61–76. Springer
7. Pérez JF, Casale G,(2013) Assessing SLA compliance from Palladio component models. In: Proceedings of the 2nd workshop on management of resources and services in cloud and sky computing (MICAS). IEEE Press

[2]Web Services Agreement Specification (WS-Agreement) http://www.ogf.org/documents/GFD.192.pdf.

8. Becker S, Koziolek H, Reussner R (2009) The Palladio component model for model-driven performance prediction. J Syst Softw 82(1):3–22
9. Franks G, Maly P, Woodside M, Petriu DC, Hubbard A (2009) Layered queueing network solver and simulator user manual. Real-Time and Distributed Systems Lab Carleton Univ Canada
10. Casale G, Tribastone M (2011) Fluid analysis of queueing in two-stage random environments. In: Eighth international conference on quantitative evaluation of systems (QEST). IEEE, pp 21–30

Chapter 5
Monitoring in a Multi-cloud Environment

Marco Miglierina and Elisabetta Di Nitto

5.1 Introduction

The Cloud brings velocity to the development and release process of applications, however software systems become complex, distributed on multiple clouds, dynamic and heterogenous, leveraging both PaaS and IaaS resources. In this context, gathering feedback on the health and usage of services becomes really hard with traditional monitoring tools, since they were built for on-premise solutions offering uniform monitoring APIs and under the assumption that the application configuration evolves slowly over time. Still, visibility via monitoring is essential to understand how the application is behaving and to enable automatic remediation features such as the ones offered by MODAClouds.

Tower 4Clouds is a monitoring platform built with multi-cloud applications in mind. It offers a model-based approach that helps the user to focus on abstract concepts when configuring the monitoring activity of complex and heterogeneous applications running on multiple clouds. Configuration is done via a powerful rule language, which allows the user to instruct the platform once, predicating on the model of the application. Within a single rule the user will be able to configure what and how data should be collected, what aggregations should be performed, what condition should be verified and what actions should be executed. Tower 4Clouds is also highly composable. Custom metrics and third party monitoring tools can be easily integrated.

M. Miglierina · E. Di Nitto (✉)
Politecnico di Milano - DEIB, Piazza L. da Vinci 32, 20133 Milano, Italy
e-mail: elisabetta.dinitto@polimi.it

M. Miglierina
e-mail: marco.miglierina@polimi.it

E. Di Nitto et al. (eds.), *Model-Driven Development and Operation of Multi-Cloud Applications*, PoliMI SpringerBriefs,
DOI 10.1007/978-3-319-46031-4_5

5.2 Tower 4Clouds Architecture

In order to address the multi-cloud requirement, we could not rely on the monitoring infrastructure provided by a specific cloud provider. We therefore developed Tower 4Clouds as an open source modular platform. Figure 5.1 depicts the general architecture of the platform.

The core elements of the architecture are *Data Analyzers* which acquire data described as RDF tuples and perform filtering, aggregation, and statistical analyses on them. They receive data from multiple *Data Collectors* that can wrap preexisting monitoring tools. Examples of preexisting tools we managed to integrate with our platform are Sigar and Collectd.

Data Analyzers produce output metrics for *Observers* that subscribe for such data. Observers can be other Data Analyzers or external tools that may support, for instance, visualization of monitoring data or the execution of some application-specific actions in response of the occurrence of some events.

The typical configuration we have experimented with includes a Deterministic Data Analyzer (DDA), in charge of performing filtering and aggregation of data, connected to Observers such as a *Statistical Data Analyzer* (SDA), which executes prediction algorithms on data, Graphite or InfluxDB for storing time series data to be then used by graphing tools such as Grafana. The DDA core is the C-SPARQL engine, a general purpose RDF stream reasoner based on the C-SPARQL language [2], which we exploited to monitor applications [3].

As we anticipated, we are not monitoring static and slowly changing systems. Cloud applications are dynamic therefore we had to provide the platform with the elasticity required to reconfigure and update its internal model according to application changes. Such elasticity is obtained by giving data collectors the responsibility

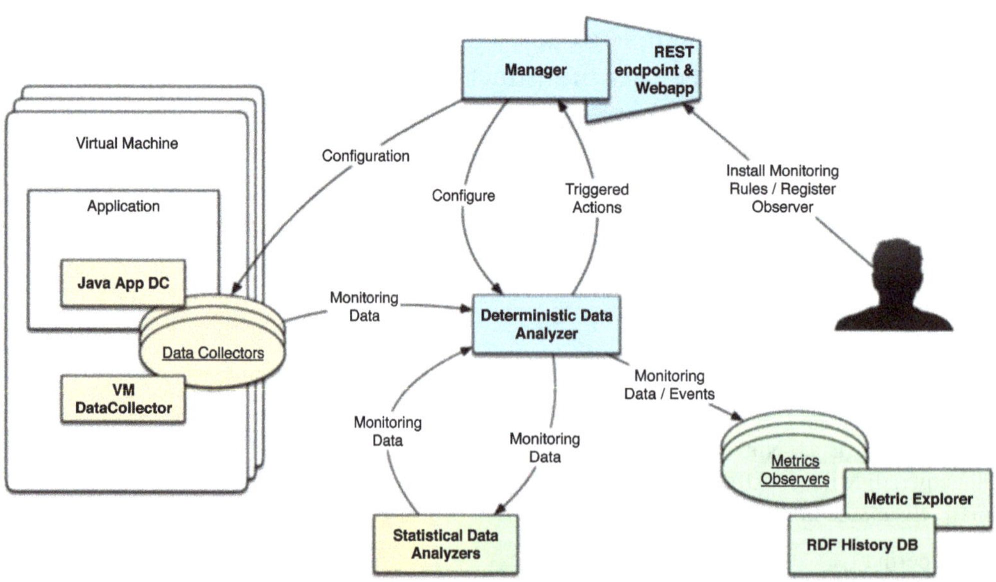

Fig. 5.1 Tower 4Clouds architecture

of registering to the central server (i.e., the Manager in Fig. 5.1) and notifying about resources they are monitoring, avoiding any central discovery mechanism. Collectors are supposed to be available as long as they periodically contact the server. After a predefined period of inactivity, the corresponding monitored resource is removed from the server internal model and considered unavailable.

Finally, we implemented a mono-directional communication protocol used by data collectors to register and to send monitoring data. Since the connection is always from data collectors to the server, there is no need to implement routing strategies and listen to ports at the client side. This allows to have fewer requirements on the XaaS services in charge of hosting the monitored application services.

5.3 Application Configuration Model

Metrics per se are dumb numbers, in order to actually understand where data is coming from and improve visibility, a model of the application is required to give semantic meaning to all its components and relationships among them. Different cloud providers, for example, are explicitly modeled so that per-cloud aggregations of data can be computed. The model, which is stored by the *Manager* component in Fig. 5.1, is maintained in sync in a distributed fashion by data collectors which are running on monitored hosts.

Figure 5.2 shows an example of model of a simple e-commerce webapp deployed on two different clouds (Flexiant and Amazon), providing 3 different methods (register, login and checkout).

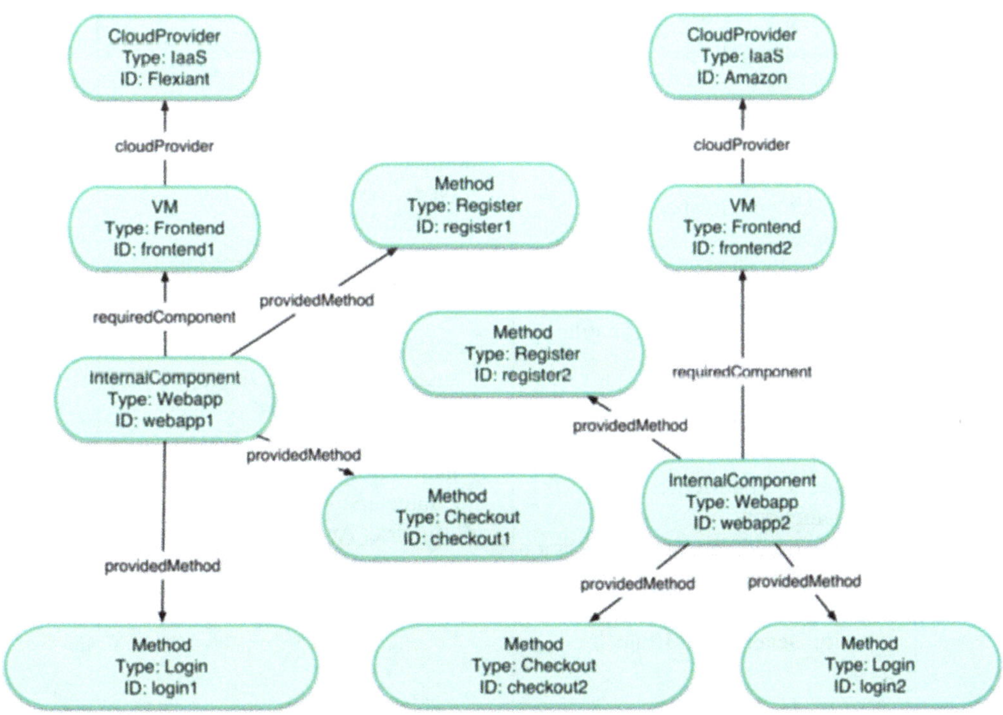

Fig. 5.2 Model example

5.4 Monitoring Rules

The configuration of the monitoring system is obtained via monitoring rules, which consist in recipes written by the QoS engineer describing the monitoring activity in a cloud-independent way. Monitoring rules can be automatically derived from QoS constraints specified during the design time and then customized according to users needs. A rule is composed of 5 building blocks:

- *monitoredTargets*, where a list of monitored resources is identified by either class, type or id;
- *collectedMetric*, where the metric to be collected is specified together with any data collector-specific parameter;
- *metricAggregation*, where the aggregation among average, percentile, sum, count, max, min of collected data is selected as well as whether the aggregation should be over all data or grouped by a specific class of resources (e.g., by cloud provider, or by vm);
- *condition*, where a condition to be verified can be expressed predicating on the aggregated value;
- *actions*, the action to be executed given the condition is satisfied (if any).

Table 5.1 Examples of monitoring rules

RTConstraint_Rule	*DetailedRAMRule*
– id: RTConstraint_Rule timeWindow: 60 timeStep: 60 enabled: true monitoredTargets: – type: Login – type: Register – type: Checkout collectedMetric: metricName: ResponseTime parameters: – samplingProbability: 1 metricAggregation: aggregateFunction: Percentile parameters: – thPercentile: 99 condition: METRIC > 10000 actions: – name: OutputMetric parameters: – metric: RTConstraint_Violation – name: EnableRule parameters: – id: DetailedRAMRule	– id: DetailedRAMRule timeWindow: 10 timeStep: 10 enabled: false monitoredTargets: – type: Frontend collectedMetric: metricName: RAMUtilization parameters: – samplingTime: 5 metricAggregation: aggregateFunction: Average groupingClass: VM actions: – name: OutputMetric parameters: – metric: AverageRAMUtilization

Table 5.1 provides two examples of rules that predicate over the example model provided in Fig. 5.2. The first rule (i.e., *RTConstraint_Rule*) instructs the platform to collect the response time of all three methods, compute the 99th percentile every 60 s, and check if it is lower than 10 s. In case the computed metric is over 10 s, the platform will produce a new metric named *RTConstraint_Violation*, which will be available as input of other rules and for observers, and will enable a second rule named *DetailedRAMRule*. This second rule is telling the platform to collect the average RAM utilization on all Frontend machines and produce a new metric named *AverageRAMUtilization* for each VM. *DetailedRAMRule* is not active in the initial monitoring configuration (in fact, its enabled attribute is set to false). This means that the data it needs are not collected. When the execution of *RTConstraint_Rule* activates it (that is, when the response time of the methods under monitoring is slow), data collectors are instructed to start sending the required metrics to the Data Analyzer that can then execute the rule. Thanks to this mechanism it is possible to increase or decrease the level of the monitoring, and the consequent overhead on the execution of the whole system, depending on the status of the system itself.

5.5 Conclusion

Tower 4Clouds is available as open source software.[1] It has been used as part of MODAClouds by all case studies owners that have been able to customize it for their purpose without a direct intervention of its main developers. Moreover, it is being used also within the SeaClouds project [1] where it has become one of the main infrastructural components. Thanks to its modularity, Tower 4Clouds has been incorporated within SeaClouds as it is, and SeaClouds partners have built around it the code needed to automatically derive monitoring rules and Data Collectors configurations from their design time specification of SeaClouds applications.

References

1. Brogi A et al (2015) CLEI Electron J 18(1):1–14
2. Barbieri DF et al (2010) C-SPARQL: a continuous query language for RDF data streams Int J Semantic Comput 4:3
3. Miglierina M et al (2013) Exploiting stream reasoning to monitor multi-cloud applications. In: 2013 ISWC 2nd international workshop on Ordering and Reasoning (OrdRing), 21–22 Oct 2013

[1] https://github.com/deib-polimi/tower4clouds.

Chapter 6
Load Balancing for Multi-cloud

Gabriel Iuhasz, Pooyan Jamshidi, Weikun Wang and Giuliano Casale

6.1 Introduction

Load balancing is an integral part of software systems that require to serve requests with multiple concurrent computing resources such as servers, clusters, network links, central processing units or disk drives. Load balancing aims to optimize resource use, maximize throughput, minimize response time, and avoid overload of any single resource. It can also lead to a higher reliability through redundant resources. Load balancing typically involves two major components: (i) a controller, a piece of software or hardware controlling the routing of requests to the backend resources according to an specific routing policy; (ii) a reasoner that determines the routing policy. The policy can be set at design-time based on the result of the reasoner or at runtime based on periodic observation of response time and throughput.

The MODAClouds Load Balancer (Fig. 6.1) is a component for dispatching requests from end users to application servers following certain load balancing policies. It consists of a load balancing controller and a reasoner. The controller extends

G. Iuhasz (✉)
Institute E-Austria Timisoara and West University of TimiŞoara,
B-dul Vasile Pârvan 4, 300223 TimiŞoara, Romania
e-mail: iuhasz.gabriel@info.uvt.ro

P. Jamshidi · W. Wang · G. Casale
Department of Computing, Imperial College London,
180 Queens Gate, SW7 2AZ London, UK
e-mail: p.jamshidi@imperial.ac.uk

W. Wang
e-mail: weikun.wang11@imperial.ac.uk

G. Casale
e-mail: g.casale@imperial.ac.uk

E. Di Nitto et al. (eds.), *Model-Driven Development and Operation of Multi-Cloud Applications*, PoliMI SpringerBriefs,
DOI 10.1007/978-3-319-46031-4_6

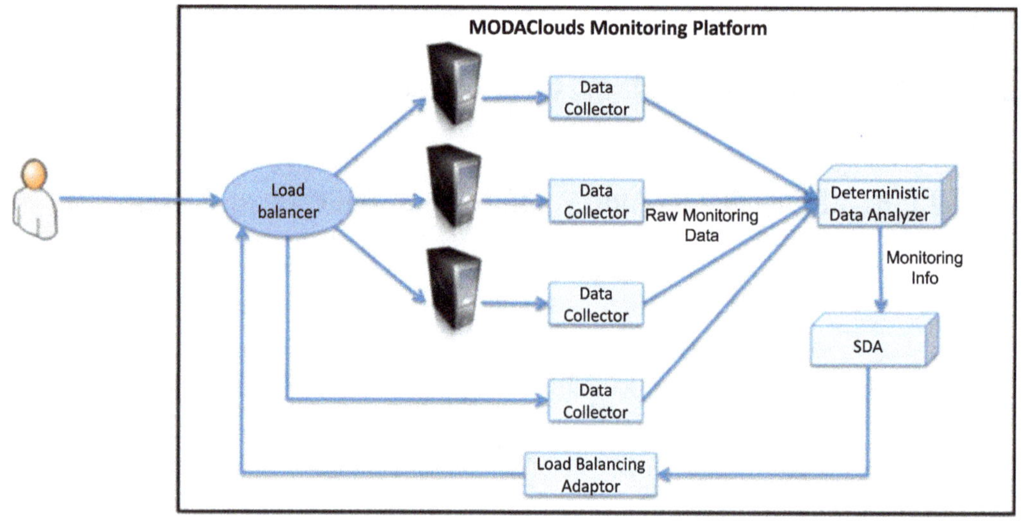

Fig. 6.1 The MODAClouds Load Balancer

well known open source load balancing and proxying for TCP and HTTP-based applications called HAProxy.[1]

6.2 Load Balancing Controller

In MODAClouds, we developed pyHrapi,[2] a set of REST APIs to interact with the core HAProxy engine. pyHrapi essentially controls the behavior of HAProxy through easy to use APIs easing the way self-adapting components of MODAClouds needs to interact with load balancing component either for configuration update or controlling its behavior at runtime.

6.3 Load Balancing Reasoner

MODAClouds Load Balancer uses the Weighted Round Robin policy, which dispatches requests to each server proportionally based on the assigned weights and in circular order. At runtime, algorithms proposed in [1] are implemented [2] to change the weights of the servers in order to optimize the revenue of the system. The revenue is defined as weighted throughput of different classes of users. The support of multiclass reasoning is useful in real applications when the users have different privileges, e.g. golden, silver and bronze, which stand for different levels of services. Such levels of service can be formalised by means of SLAs. In the reasoner component, the

[1] http://www.haproxy.org/.

[2] https://github.com/ieat/MODAClouds-loadbalancer-controller.

calculation of throughput and response time is based on log data analysis of the load balancing controller. At runtime, the per request logs are accumulated in the load balancing controller log file based on the requests hitting backend resources.

Data collector In order to observe the change of the system, we have developed a log file collector for Haproxy. This log file collector continuously extracts information from the log based on a predefined regular expression. Metrics like response time, arrival and departure time-stamps, request type and session IDs are particularly useful for the load balancing analysis to examine the processing requirement of each type of request on different types of servers. This Haproxy log data collector is integrated into Tower 4Clouds (see Chap. 5) and sends data to the Deterministic Data Analyzer (DDA) component.

Demand estimation The logs collected from the Haproxy log data collector are sent to the Haproxy specific demand estimation SDA from the DDA for analysis. We have developed two Haproxy specific demand estimation SDAs to obtain the demands of different classes of users: Complete Information (CI) and Utilization-based Regression (UBR). The CI method requires both the arrival time-stamps and departure time-stamps of each requests. The UBR, on the other hand, needs CPU utilization on the application server as well as the throughput of the requests. The demands obtained from either SDA will be used by the Load balancing adaptor to obtain the optimal weights for each backend resources.

In particular, we obtain the demand of different classes of users by evaluating the requests they send during one session. Here, we assume users have a similar behaviour for sending the requests. We achieve this by grouping the requests by the session IDs and examine if there are common requests among different sessions.

6.4 Multi-cloud Load Balancing

Local Load Balancing (LLB), also called cluster-level load balancing or intra-Cloud load balancing (see previous section), provides load balancing between VMs, which are inside a Cloud service or a virtual network (VNet) within a regional zone. However, there are several motivations for multi-Cloud (inter-Cloud) load balancing:

- *Failover*: An organization intends to provide highly reliable services for its customers. This can be realized by figuring out backup services in case their primary service goes down. A common architectural pattern for service failover is to provide a set of identical interfaces and route service requests to a primary service endpoint, with a list of one or more replicated ones. If the primary service goes down for a reason, requesting clients are routed to the other Cloud.
- *Gradual enhancement/graceful degradation*: Allocate a percentage of traffic to route to a new interface, and gradually shift the traffic over time.
- *Application migration to another Cloud*: A profile can be setup with both primary and secondary interfaces, and a weight can be specified to route the requests to each interface.

- *Cloud bursting*: A Cloud service can be expanded into another private or public Cloud by putting it behind a multi-Cloud load balancer profile. Once there is a need for extra resources, it can be added (or dynamically removed) and specify what proportion of requests goes to newly provisioned resources.
- *Internet scale services*: In order to load balance endpoints that are located in different Clouds across the world, one can direct incoming traffic to the closest port in terms of the lowest latency, which typically corresponds to the shortest geographic distance.
- *Fault tolerance*. A fault tolerant Cloud application detect failed components and fail over to another Cloud until a failure is resolved. It not only depends on deployment strategies but also on application level design strategies, for example, a reliable application may degraded and partly route the request to another Cloud at the same time.

6.4.1 Usage Scenario of Multi-cloud Load Balancing

Once a failure in a Cloud occurs, traffic can be redirected to VMs running in another Cloud. Multi-Cloud load balancing can facilitate this task. It allows to automatically manage the failover of traffic to another Cloud in case the primary Cloud fails. When configuring multi-Cloud load balancing, we need to provide a new global load balancer in front of the local ones in each Cloud. Global load balancer abstracts load balancing one level up the local level. The global load balancer maps to all the deployments it manages. Within global load balancer, the weights for the load balancing policy determine the priority of the deployments that users will be routed to a deployment. The global load balancer monitors the endpoints of the deployments and notes when a deployment in specific Cloud fails. At failure, global load balancer reasoner will change the weights and route users to other Cloud (Fig. 6.2).

6.5 Load Balancing and Failure Management

A requirement for the runtime platform is to be robust in case of failures of individual components. In particular, a failure of the load balancer could cause a major loss of connectivity for an entire cluster of machines. To prevent this situation, it is needed to replicate the load balancer and initiate an automatic fail-over switch to the backup load balancer in case the main load-balancer fails.

In MODAClouds, we use Trigger technology to handle load balancer failure. Triggers are functions that allow an action in Cloud Orchestrator to initiate a second action. A trigger is written as a block of code that run either before an event occurs (a pre trigger) or after an event occurs (a post trigger). One advantage is that a pool of images can be created and automatically started in the event of a fault. This reduces the requirement for a System Administrator to be involved and as a result reduce

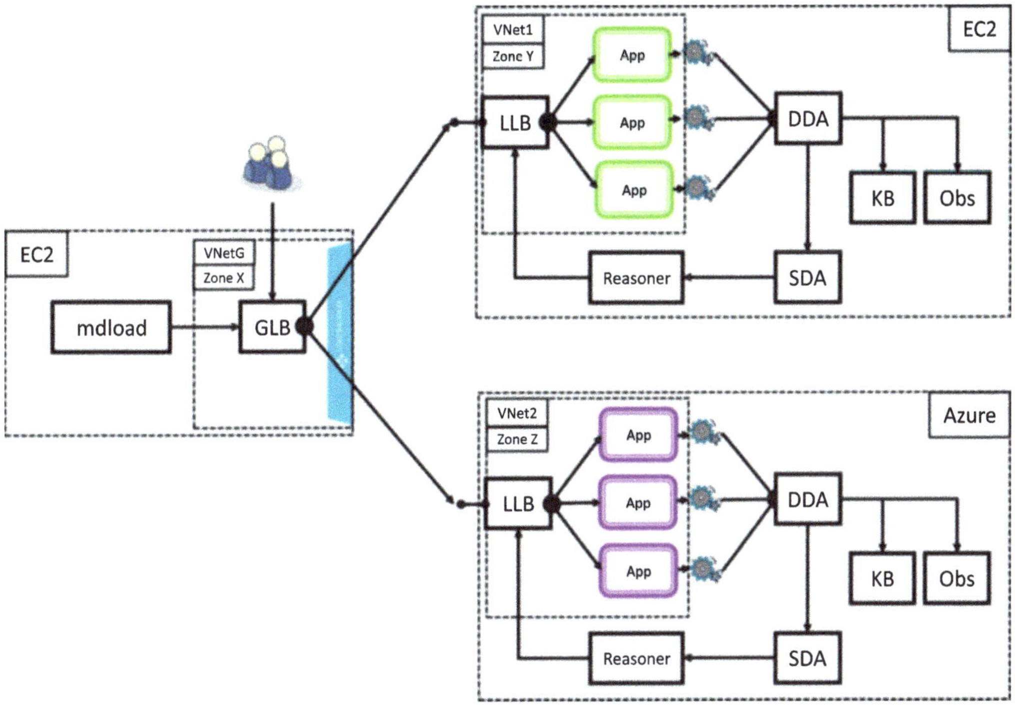

Fig. 6.2 Overview of multi-Cloud load balancing in MODAClouds

the overhead cost as well as providing a fast automatic response. Also as a snapshot of a disk is taken, if required a roll back in the event of changes or faults can be quick using this taken snapshot and the provided tools. We also use triggers to add the newly started VM into the load balancer, that would work in conjunction with the previously created triggers. In the experiments we performed we exploited the trigger implementation presented in Chap. 15.

6.6 Conclusion

The observations with our experimental study can be summarized as follows:

- *Flexible load balancing*. The approach enabled adaptive changes in the weights according to the heterogeneity of the resources in each Cloud.
- *Reduce application downtime*. The approach improved the availability of Cloud-based applications by automatically directing user access to a new location anytime there is a congestion in a Cloud.
- *Improved performance*. The approach made application more responsive by directing access to an application according to the weights

Further details on implementation, experimental results, and the interconnection with the other runtime components of MODAClouds can be found in [3].

References

1. Anselmi J, Casale G (2013) Heavy-traffic revenue maximization in parallel multiclass queues. Perform Eval
2. Wang W, Casale G (2014) Evaluating weighted round robin load balancing for cloud web services
3. Iuhasz G et al (2015) Runtime environment final release. Modaclouds Deliverable D6.5.3

Chapter 7
Fault-Tolerant Off-line Data Migration: The Hegira4Clouds Approach

Elisabetta Di Nitto and Marco Scavuzzo

7.1 Introduction

The Cloud offers the potential to support high scalability of applications. An increase in the application workload is typically handled by triggering the replication of its components so as to increase the application computational capability offered to users. Moreover, an increase in the amount of data to be handled can be easily managed by exploiting scalable DBMSs supporting partitioning of data on different nodes. These are the so called NoSQL databases that have been specifically built to offer scalability, high availability of data and tolerance to network partitions [9].

Unfortunately, when looking more closely at how NoSQL databases work, one realizes that they represent a good solution for scalability, but they do not offer mechanisms to allow migration among data stored in NoSQLs from different vendors. More specifically, data migration is not a new problem per se. It is a well established topic in relational databases world; this is mainly due to the standardization occurred at the data model level (with DDL) and at query level (with DML and DQL). There exist several tools (see, e.g., [2, 4, 6, 7]) which allow to migrate data across relational databases and, thanks to SQL, it is possible to preserve queries, compliant to the standard, even after the migration. On the contrary, in the NoSQL database field there exist no standard neither for interfaces nor for the data models and, as such, to the best of our knowledge, there are no tools which allow to perform data migration across different NoSQLs. Some databases provide tools to extract data from them (e.g., Google Bulkloader [3]), but in the end, it is up to the programmer to actually map those data to the target database data model and perform the migration.

E. Di Nitto (✉) · M. Scavuzzo
Politecnico di Milano - DEIB, Piazza L. da Vinci 32, 20133 Milano, Italy
e-mail: elisabetta.dinitto@polimi.it

M. Scavuzzo
e-mail: marco.scavuzzo@polimi.it

E. Di Nitto et al. (eds.), *Model-Driven Development and Operation of Multi-Cloud Applications*, PoliMI SpringerBriefs,
DOI 10.1007/978-3-319-46031-4_7

With our approach, that we call Hegira4Clouds,[1] we aim at providing a solution to the data migration problem in the context of NoSQL databases, trying to preserve, at the same time, the specific properties characterizing each NoSQL database. For the moment, we focus on column-family databases as they are among the most interesting class of NoSQL for their high level of scalability. Hegira4Clouds migration approach is based on the idea of extracting data from the source database, transforming them into an intermediate format, and, finally, translate and store them into the target database. Data transfer is fault tolerant as it enables the correct termination of the migration even in the presence of a failure within the migration infrastructure.

In the following of this chapter, we briefly present Hegira4Clouds intermediate format (Sect. 7.2) and its architecture, focusing, in particular, on the fault tolerance features (Sect. 7.3). Finally, we evaluate the approach (Sect. 7.4) and discuss conclusions and future work (Sect. 7.5).

7.2 Hegira4Clouds Intermediate Meta-Model

The Hegira4Clouds intermediate format is defined by an *intermediate meta-model* described in detail in [13]. It takes into account the features of the most widely used NoSQL and we have shown that it is sufficiently general for dealing with the features of so-called columnar and key-value NoSQL databases [8, 15]. Thanks to its definition, the adoption of a new NoSQL system in Hegira4Clouds requires only the development of the translator from this new NoSQL into the intermediate format and vice versa. Furthermore, thanks to this intermediate meta-model, Hegira4Clouds is able to preserve the data types, read consistency policies, and secondary indexes supported by the source database.

In particular, we preserve data types by keeping track of the type of each migrated data explicitly, even though that type is not available in the destination database. This is accomplished by performing the following procedure: data converted into the intermediate format are always serialized into a *property value field* and the original data type is stored as a string into a *property type field*. When data are converted from the intermediate format into the target one, if the destination database supports that particular data type, the value is deserialized. Otherwise, the value is kept serialized and it is up to the application level to correctly interpret (deserialize) the value according to the type field.

As extensively detailed in [10, 13], read consistency policies are handled through the concept of *Partition Group* (Fig. 7.1). Entities that require strong consistency on read operations will be assigned, in the intermediate format, to the same Partition Group value. Entities managed according to an eventual consistency policy will be assigned to different Partition Group values. When entities share the same Partition Group, if the target database supports strongly consistent read operations,

[1]Repository: https://github.com/deib-polimi/hegira-components/.

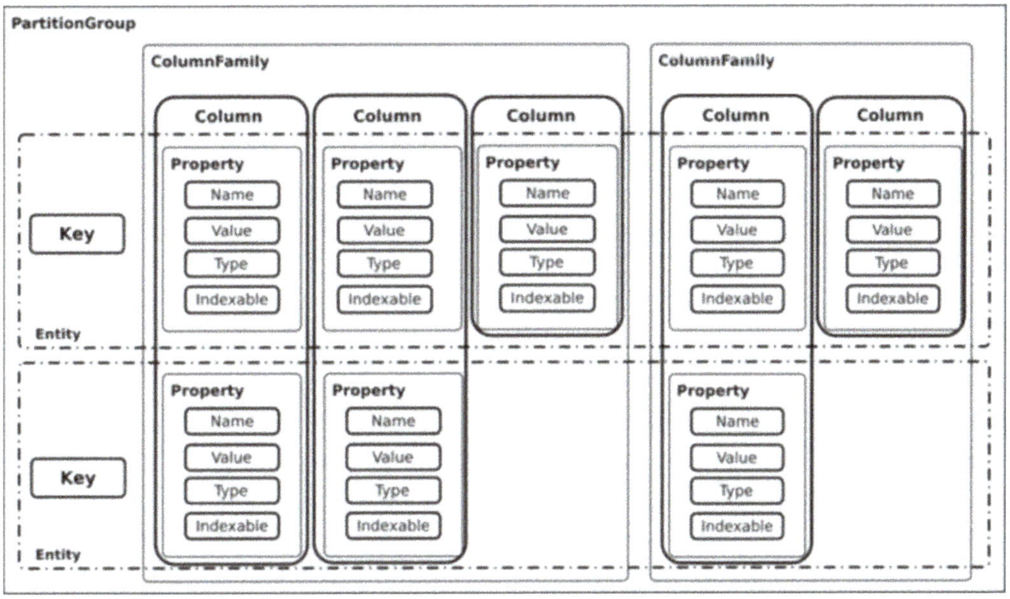

Fig. 7.1 Intermediate meta-model

then Hegira4Clouds adapts data accordingly (depending on the target database data-model). Otherwise, Hegira4Clouds simply persists the data so as that they will be read in an eventual consistent way, and creates an auxiliary data structure to preserve the consistency information.

Finally, secondary indexes are preserved across different database by means of the property *indexable field*. More specifically, during the conversion into the intermediate format, if a certain property needs to be indexed, it is marked as indexable. When converting into the target format, if the target database supports secondary indexes, the property is mapped consequently according to the specific interfaces provided by the target database. Otherwise, Hegira4Clouds creates an auxiliary data structure on the target database which stores the references to the indexed properties, so that, when migrating again these data to another database supporting secondary indexes, they can be properly reconstructed.

7.3 Architecture and Fault Tolerance Features

The Hegira4Clouds architecture is shown in Fig. 7.2. To provide scalablity and reliability, each component is decoupled from the other, and the interacting components communicate by means of a distributed queue. A *Source Reading Component (SRC)* extracts data from the source database, one entity at a time or in batch (if the source database supports batch operations) translates data into the intermediate format, by means of the respective *direct translator*, and puts the data in the *Metamodel queue*.

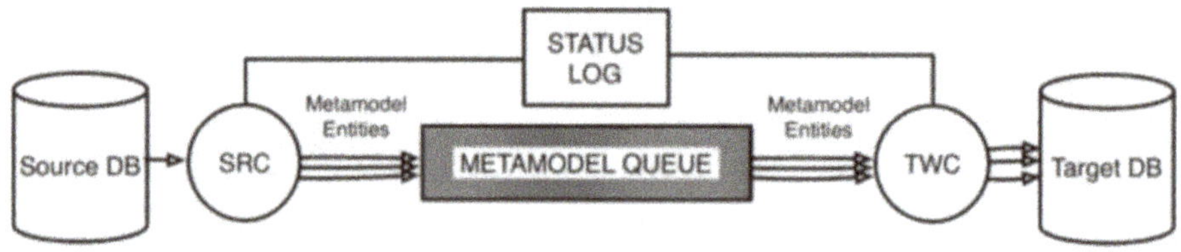

Fig. 7.2 Hegira4Clouds data migration architecture

This queue temporarily stores the data produced by the SRC so that other components can consume them at their own peace, thus allowing the system to cope with the different throughputs of the source and target databases. In parallel, a *Target Writing Component (TWC)* consumes the data from the queue and converts them into the target database data-model, thanks to an *inverse translator* (specific for each supported database). After conversion the data is stored in the target database. Hence the role of translators is that of mapping data back and forth between the source/target database and the intermediate format, performing the (de)serializations, checking for data types support, properly mapping indexes and adapting the data to preserve different read consistency policies. Two examples of translators (Google Datastore and Azure Tables) are extensively described in [10, 13]. SRC and TWC are organized in threads called *Source Reading Threads (SRT)* and *Target Writing Threads (TWT)*, respectively to achieve the maximum possible throughput.

Hegira4Clouds fault tolerance focuses on tolerating both databases reading/writing errors and outages (i.e., external faults) as well as crashes in the components of the migration system (i.e., internal faults).

Queue faults may be prevented by adopting a distributed, disk-persisted, queuing mechanism, so by assuming that this queue is able to automatically recover from faults of its replicas (that is the reason why we a adopt RabbitMQ, widely used in production environments).

Writing errors on the target database are addressed by the Metamodel queue; in particular, TWTs synchronously write data on the target database and send acknowledgment messages to the queue if the data were persisted correctly; only at this point, acknowledged data are removed from the queue. Thus, if an error occurs on the target database, another TWT (or a new TWC) can take over the specific write operations.

Reacting to reading errors in presence of faults on the source database, instead, is more difficult because of the heterogeneity of the different NoSQL databases; while some databases guarantee an absolute pointer to the data even after an error or a crash, thus enabling the possibility to restart the migration from the exact point in which it has been interrupted, some others (e.g., Google Datastore) do not.

Our approach to avoid restarting the migration from scratch consists in virtually partitioning the data in the source database, so that partitions containing a certain amount of data to be migrated can be retrieved in an ordered and unambiguous way, independently from the source NoSQL database that is being used. In this way, if there is an unrecoverable database error (i.e.,m external fault) or if the SRC crashes (i.e., internal fault), the migration can start from the last retrieved partition. This approach has been initially presented in [11] and is presented and evaluated in detail in the rest of this chapter. Of course, such an approach implies that data are stored in the databases according to a custom design. For this reason, Hegira4Clouds also supports a design-agnostic approach (see [14]) that is compatible with any kind of data design, but it is not able to react to unrecoverable source database faults or SRC faults (i.e., an internal fault).

7.3.1 Virtual Data Partitioning

Since the source database may not support absolute pointers to the data, in order to keep track of data that is being migrated, there must be some sort of shared knowledge between the application and Hegira4Clouds. For this reason, we define the concept of Virtual Data Partition (VDP), which is a logical grouping of entities contained in the source database. By making the assumption that the applications, using the source database, insert entities according to a sequential incremented (primary) key, it is possible to track the point where a data migration task was interrupted. In fact, by applying this technique, and storing only the last generated sequential id (*lastSeqNr*), it possible to unequivocally create VDPs and associate stored entities with them; in fact, by using an approach similar to paged virtual memory (virtual memory management) for operating systems, it is possible to map an ordered set of entities to a VDP (i.e., Eq. 7.2) and viceversa (i.e., Eq. 7.3).

To determine, at migration-time, the exact number of VDPs based on the last generated sequence number (*lastSeqNr*) and the user-defined partition size (*PS*) we use Eq. 7.1.

$$\#partitions = \left\lceil lastSeqNr/PS \right\rceil \tag{7.1}$$

$$VDPid_k = \left\lfloor key_{x,k}/PS \right\rfloor \tag{7.2}$$

We use Eq. 7.2 to calculate the id of the VDP containing the given entity (identified by its key, i.e., $key_{x,k}$). Finally, Eq. 7.3 can be used to calculate the first and last entity keys belonging to a given VDP (i.e., $VDPid_k$). Notice that:

$$\begin{aligned} key_{1,k} &= VDPid_k \times PS \\ &\vdots \\ key_{n,k} &= [(VDPid_k + 1) \times PS] - 1 \end{aligned} \tag{7.3}$$

- Since entities are inserted into the source database according to a sequential incremented key (generated in order to guarantee the global total order of the id), the entities contained in each VDP are ordered.

- The number of the VDPs is not fixed a priori, but it grows together with the inserted entities, and it is a factor of the number of inserted entities (*lastSeqNr*) and the maximum number of entities VDPs can contain (i.e., *PS*).
- The size of the VDPs, in terms of contained entities (and thus the number of VDPs, Eq. 7.1), can be determined at migration-time (by fixing a value for *PS*) and it can change from one migration to another, without affecting stored data.

Hence, for migrating data according to this approach, it suffices to read the last generated sequential number from a fault-tolerant, distributed storage, i.e., the *status log*, and decide the VDPs proper size; once done so, for each VDP, the SRC extracts the entities, from the source database, and executes the migration task.

If the source database supports range scan queries (e.g., HBase, Cassandra) it is possible, for each database specific *translator*, to request all the range of entities contained in a VDP, for example $VDPid_2$, with a single query, just by specifying its first (i.e., $key_{1,2}$) and last (i.e., $key_{n,2}$) entity keys. Otherwise, if the source database does not support range queries, the specific database *translator* requests each entity, contained in the VDP, one by one. In the first case, entities retrieval from the source database, is much faster than in the second case, because only a request, towards the database, is issued; while, in the second case, exactly *PS* requests are sent to the source database.

The limit of the VDP approach is that VDPs might also contain the ids of previously erased entities; while on the first hand, in case of range scans, this does not affect the performance of the migration task, since the source database handles missing entities in a range; on the other hand, if the source database does not support range scans, and the SRC has to issue a request per each entity contained in the VDP, the source database will return an error when trying to retrieve a previously deleted entity. The SRC skips the deleted entities that generate an error, but issuing queries also for deleted entities slows down the migration task. In the worst case, i.e., when all of the entities in a VDP have been erased, there may be a severe drop on the data migration overall throughput.

In order to keep track of the *migration status* (i.e., the number of entities correctly migrated towards the target database) and to allow for data synchronization (discussed in [12]), Hegira4Clouds exploits the VDPs. In particular, when the SRC is instructed to begin a migration task, it creates a *snapshot* of the source database, which is stored in the status log. A snapshot consists of: (a) a list of all the VDPs at the time the migration task was started (which depends on the value of *PS*, selected when the migration command was issued); (b) the status of each VDP, which can be of four types: "not migrated", "under migration", "migrated" and "synch"; (c) the last sequence number issued at the time the migration task was started.

When creating the snapshot, every VDP status is set to "not migrated". Once the SRC starts to extract the entities relative to a given VDP, it sets the status of that VDP to "under migration". When a TWT determines it has processed all entities relative to a given VDP, it sets that particular VDP status to "migrated". The "synch" VDP status is used when a partition is being synchronized, but this is out of the scope of this chapter. A TWT is able to determine if a VDP has completely been processed by counting the effective number of processed entities for that VDP and comparing it with the number of entities the VDP actually contains (piggybacked on each metamodel entity and specific to different VDPs). Hence, each time a TWT processes an entity relative to a given VDP, it increments an associated counter; if the counter reaches the value piggybacked in those metamodel entities, then the TWT changes the VDP status to "migrated". In this way all Hegira4Clouds components are aware of the migration status at any point in time, and can therefore take the appropriate decisions in case of faults (and also of data synchronization, as described in [12]). Additional details about the snapshot management are provided in [14].

7.3.2 Recovering from Faults

Hegira4Clouds recovery approach assumes that there exists an external orchestrator (e.g., Mesosphere DCOS [5]) that acts as follows:

1. it monitors the statuses of Hegira4Clouds components, i.e., the SRC and the TWC;
2. if it detects a fault on the SRC, it waits until the TWC finishes to process all the messages in the Metamodel queue and starts a new SRC;
3. if it detects a fault on the TWC, it stops the SRC from reading data from the source database and restarts both components.
4. Once the components have been restarted, the orchestrator calls Hegira4Clouds recovery API.

Hegira4Clouds components, upon receiving a recovery command, in order to avoid inconsistencies during data migration, empty the Metamodel queue. Then, each components act as follows:

- the SRC
  - downloads the migration status from the status log;
  - for those VDPs whose status is "under migration", the SRC changes it to "not migrate" (this prevents inconsistencies from happening);
  - finally, it starts to extract data from the source database starting from the first VDP whose status is "not migrated".
- the TWC, just waits for the Metamodel queue to be filled by the SRC.

7.4 Evaluation: Migrating Tweets

This section evaluates Hegira4Clouds using a large data set extracted from Twitter. In particular, we stored into GAE Datastore 10,693,800 publicly available tweets [1] and then we ran Hegira4Clouds to migrate them into Azure Tables. The purpose of the experiment is to check if Hegira4Clouds is able to perform the partitioned data migration with an acceptable overhead (w.r.t. to the standard data migration [14]) and without introducing errors directly due to the migration process.

Experimental setup As mentioned before, our data set was composed of 10,693,800 tweets. Each tweet, in addition to the 140 characters long message, contains also details about the user, creation date, geospatial information, etc. Each tweet was stored in GAE Datastore as a single entity, with an extra sequential identifier (according to the specifics reported in Sect. 7.3.1) and a variable number of properties (with different data types). On average, each tweet on GAE Datastore was 3.05 KB. The total entities size was 31.1 GB. We tested Hegira4Clouds in two different scenarios:

1. *Standalone environent*: all of the migration system components, including the queue (RabbitMQ 3.4.6) and the status log (Apache ZooKeeper 3.5.4), were deployed inside an Azure VM.
2. *Distributed environent*: two equally-sized VMs in the same virtual network, one hosting the SRC, the TWC and the web-server exposing the REST APIs, and the other equipped with the queue and the status log.

In both scenarios the VMs were configured as follows: Ubuntu Server 12.04, located in Microsoft WE data center, with 4 CPU cores and 7 GB RAM.

Scenario 1: Standalone environment This test migrated data described above and used 32 TWTs to write data in parallel on Azure Tables and 8 SRTs to read data in parallel from Google Datastore. The main measured system metrics were (a) the total migration time and consequently the migration throughput (measured in entities per second), (b) the time needed by the SRC to extract the entities from the source database, convert and put them in the queue, and (c) the overall CPU utilization relative to all Hegira4Clouds components. We performed three different runs and computed the average of each metric. Moreover, in order to evaluate how predictable each run was with this configuration, we also computed the standard deviation for each metric (Table 7.1).

Scenario 2: Distributed environment In this scenario the environment setup was composed by two equally-sized VM, one, hegira1, executing an instance of RabbitMQ and ZooKeeper, the other, hegira2, hosting the SRC and TWC components, as well as the web-server exposing the REST APIs. The migrated data and the configuration parameters were the same of the previous scenario, but, additionally, we distinguished the CPU usages of the two VMs (Table 7.2).

Table 7.1 Partitioned data migration with standalone environment

# Run	Mig. time (s)	Mig. throughput (ent/s)	Ext. time (s)	Ext. throughput (ent/s)	%CPU used
1	13470	793.90	13469	793.96	49.4
2	16882	633.44	16880	633.52	49.02
3	17486	611.56	15248	701.32	38.46
Averages	15946	670.63	15199	703.58	45.63
Std. dev.	2165.44	99.56	1706.03	80.54	6.21

Table 7.2 Partitioned data migration with distributed environment

# Run	Mig. time (s)	Mig. throughput (ent/s)	Ext. time (s)	Ext. throughput (ent/s)	%CPU used hegira 1	%CPU used hegira 2
1	12075	885.61	12073	885.76	11.1	26.99
2	12187	877.47	12183	877.76	13.05	25.7
3	13995	764.11	13993	764.22	10.06	25.11
Averages	12752.33	838.58	12749.67	838.75	11.40	25.93
Std. Dev	1077.64	67.92	1078.16	67.98	1.52	0.96

7.5 Discussion and Conclusion

From the analysis of results we can conclude that Hegira4Clouds is suitable to handle and process huge quantities of data with a very high throughput. Deploying Hegira4Clouds on a distributed environment grants higher throughput; in fact, in scenario 2, the average migration time was almost 1 hour less and consequently the migration throughput was almost 170 ent/s faster. Moreover, by looking at the standard deviations, we can conclude that distributing Hegira4Clouds components has the benefit of providing more predictable migration performance. In fact, while in the first scenario we observe an average standard deviation corresponding almost to the 15 %, in the second scenario the standard deviation is almost halved to the 8 %.

Finally, by comparing the results obtained in Scenario 2 with those of the standard (i.e., non-partitioned) data migration [14] we can assert that the performance are almost the same and the adoption of the virtual data partitioning mechanism (together with the usage of a status log, i.e., ZooKeeper) has no tangible overhead on Hegira4Clouds.

The work on Hegira4Clouds is now focusing on how to manage synchronization between database replicas and on how to support data migration while the application using such data is continuing its normal execution.

References

1. ArchiveTeam (2012) Twitter Stream https://ia601605.us.archive.org/10/items/archiveteam-twitter-stream-2012-12/archiveteam-twitter-2012-12.tar
2. Flyway https://github.com/flyway/flyway
3. Google Bulkloader, https://chromium.googlesource.com/external/googleappengine/python/+/200fcb767bdc358a3acb5cf7cad1376fe69f12c5/google/appengine/tools/bulkloader.py
4. LiquiBase, http://www.liquibase.org
5. Mesosphere, https://mesosphere.com/
6. Mysql workbench: Database migration, http://www.mysql.it/products/workbench/migrate/
7. Oracle SQL Developer Migration, http://www.oracle.com/technetwork/database/migration/index-084442.html

8. Popescu A (2010, 02) Nosql at codemash—an interesting nosql categorization. http://nosql.mypopescu.com/post/396337069/presentation-nosql-codemash-an-interesting-nosql
9. Sadalage PJ, Fowler M (2012) NoSQL Distilled: a brief guide to the emerging world of polyglot persistence. Addison-Wesley Professional
10. Scavuzzo M (2013) Interoperable data migration between NoSQL columnar databases. Master's thesis, Politecnico di Milano
11. Scavuzzo M, Di Nitto E, Ardagna D Experiences and challenges in building a data intensive system for data migration
12. Scavuzzo M, Di Nitto E, Dominiak J (2015) Data synchronisation layer. MODAClouds deliverable D6.7, April 2015. http://www.modaclouds.eu/wp-content/uploads/2012/09/MODAClouds_D6.7_DataSynchronizationLayer.pdf
13. Scavuzzo M, Nitto ED, Ceri S (2014) Interoperable data migration between nosql columnar databases. In: Grossmann G, Hallé S, Karastoyanova D, Reichert M, Rinderle-Ma S (eds) 18th IEEE international enterprise distributed object computing conference workshops and demonstrations, EDOC Workshops 2014, Ulm, Germany, 1–2 Sep 2014. IEEE, pp. 154–162. http://dx.doi.org/10.1109/EDOCW.2014.32
14. Scavuzzo M, Tamburri DA, Di Nitto E (2016) Providing big data applications with fault-tolerant data migration across heterogeneous NoSQL databases. In:Proceedings of the 2nd international workshop on BIG Data Software Engineering (BIGDSE '16). ACM, New York, NY, USA, pp 26–32
15. Scoffield B (2014) Nosql—death to relational databases(?), January 2010, presentation at the CodeMash conference in Sandusky (Ohio), 14 Jan 2014. http://www.slideshare.net/bscofield/nosql-codemash-2010

Chapter 8
Deployment of Cloud Supporting Services

Gabriel Iuhasz, Silviu Panica, Ciprian Crăciun and Dana Petcu

8.1 Introduction

The main emphasis in this chapter is on the various supporting services needed to run an application. In the MODAClouds context, all services and resources involved in running and managing an application on a given Cloud provider comprise the runtime environment.

We give an overview of the Execution Platform (Energizer 4Clouds) and its main components and services that have a direct role in deploying the supporting services. In particular we will detail the mOS operating system and its main subsystems as well as the supporting services. We briefly talk about how all services are packaged and deployed after which we give an overview of and rational behind their design and implementation. These supporting services are: **Object Store**, **Artifact Repository**, **Load-Balancer Controller** and finally the **Batch Engine**. A brief overview of how the supporting services are used in the MODAClouds project will be covered at the end of this chapter. We also cover the runtime platform integration and interdependencies of the supporting services and various other platforms that comprise the runtime platform.

G. Iuhasz (✉) · S. Panica · C. Crăciun · D. Petcu
Institute e-Austria Timisoara, West University of Timişoara,
B-dul Vasile Pârvan 4, 300223 Timişoara, Romania
e-mail: iuhasz.gabriel@info.uvt.ro

S. Panica
e-mail: silviu@info.uvt.ro

C. Crăciun
e-mail: ccraciun@info.uvt.ro

D. Petcu
e-mail: petcu@info.uvt.ro

E. Di Nitto et al. (eds.), *Model-Driven Development and Operation of Multi-Cloud Applications*, PoliMI SpringerBriefs,
DOI 10.1007/978-3-319-46031-4_8

8.2 MODAClouds Execution Platform

In this section we focus on the functionalities of the execution platform, and more precisely on the supporting services which enable the deployment and execution of various other services that are part of the runtime platform. In particular the runtime platform is responsible for monitoring and self-adaptation.

Figure 8.1 offers a general overview of the overall dependencies between the execution platform, the monitoring (Tower 4Clouds), adaptation (SpaceOps 4Clouds)

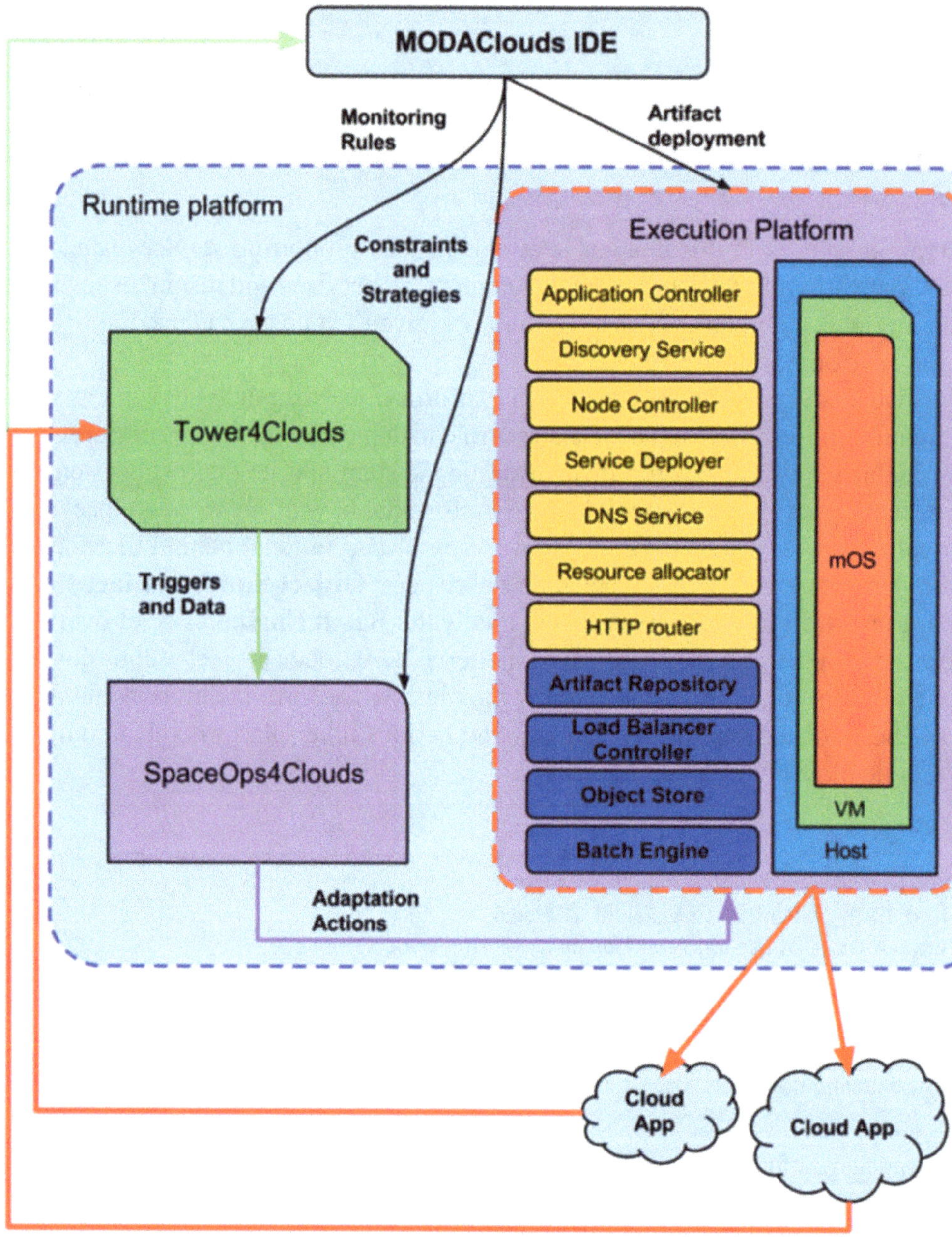

Fig. 8.1 Energizer 4Clouds—Execution Platform

and the MODACloud IDE. The execution platform has three main sub-systems; infrastructure, coordination, platform. The infrastructures sub-system handles low-level management of Cloud resources, coordination sub-system enables services to find one another and exchange messages and finally the platform sub-system handles the MODAClouds-specific tasks. The supporting services which are the main focus of this chapter can be found at the bottom of the above figure.

Discovery is an important functionality, required by all services from the execution platform. Each component consumes or provides various services, which are accessed in almost all cases over established networks protocols (HTTP, AMQP, raw TCP etc.). Thus, the developer is provided with API's that abstracts and expose these service endpoints and the way to resolve them.

8.2.1 mOS

The mOS operating system is based on existing open-source operating systems and it is used to host the MODAClouds Platform. Currently there are two versions mOS v0.x (based on Slitaz) and v1.X (based on OpenSUSE) [4]. It is designed to run on any compatible Cloud infrastructure. The pre-compiled kernels are available to support major Cloud providers such as Amazon EC2, Google Compute Engine and Flexiscale to name but a few.

There are several important services that run inside mOS which are paramount to its functioning. The mOS bootstrap service is tasked with customizing the execution platform by starting required services at boot time. These services are in charge of various actions that create the run-time environment. Other notable services are the so-called ZeroConf services which are special services hosted by the Cloud providers to enable the interaction between active VMs and a special service in order to obtain information about specific resource. The information about the resources include: user-data specified when the instance is configured at start-up, password-less SSH public key, username and password pairs, network information.

VM resource registration is handled by the naming service which generates unique name randomly and registers it with the DNS. There are other services such as user-data service, package daemon and logging service which are responsible for user scripts, package installation and event logging. The implementation of mOS v1.X using openSUSE 13.1 uses the default ramdisk for boot with slight modifications in order to satisfies some requirements by the MODAClouds platform.

8.2.2 Platform Sub-systems

The run-time bootstrapper coordinates the deployment of the core packages as well as the supporting service packages. This is achieved by delegating most of the jobs to other subsystem. It serves as a kind of frontend for the operator and the service deployment. It delegates most task to the resource allocator, node bootstrapper and controller, service deployer and finally the application deployer.

All of the above mentioned systems are crucial to the runtime. However, the main focus of this chapter is to detail the importance of supporting service for the MODAClouds runtime. Keeping this in mind, only some of the components used in the deployment of the supporting service are highlighted here. For example, the **node bootstrapper** is in charge of the initial mOS customization for the MODAClouds run-time environment. It runs as a local OS service, started at boot time or run time. It also applies all customization needed to start the runtime environment. The **node controller** is responsible with the management of the core services that runs mOS and supports the MODAClouds platform. It will start/stop and monitor the services to ensure that every main component of the execution platform is working as expected.

8.3 Supporting Services

The auto-discovery of services, previously mentioned in Sect. 8.2, depends to a large extent on the correct packaging and deployment of services. In order to run a service on the platform there are certain requirements that need to be met by the software. First, the software has to be packaged as an RPM which contains everything the service needs in order to run. These RPM packages can be made using the JSON based MODAClouds mOS Packager [5] or using the standard RPMSPEC for OpenSUSE 13 for x86_64. Any non standard dependencies must be provided together with RPM so that they can be published together in the MODAClouds repository. It is important to note that although specially designed for MODAClouds each supporting service is a standalone deployable tool outside the MODAClouds context.

In order to successfully deploy any service or component their runtime dependencies in term of other services must be specified. For example, the DDA (Deterministic Data Analyzer) tool depends at runtime on C-SPARQL. In addition, all TCP or UDP sockets on which the services listen must be specified. Finally, wrapper scripts are configuring through environmental variables the socket addresses on which services are allowed to listen and the remote service endpoints on which the service depends on.

The next subsections detail the most important supporting services from MODAClouds. These are integral for the correct functioning of the MODAClouds solution.

8.3.1 Object Store

The classic approach in software configuration is through configuration files which reside on the local disk, however such an approach is not very well suited for a Cloud environment, where VM's are started from identical templates (the VM images), and in most cases unattended, thus the configuration files must be rewritten at startup.

Luckily, for such a scenario, there are existing solutions, such as Puppet[1] or Chef.[2] However they also require a central database where the actual configuration parameters are stored. Moreover some of the deployed services might also want to store small state data, either for later retrieval, or for weak synchronization within a cluster. In this case the simplest solution is to use either a kind of database, or a distributed file system. This is the rational behind the development of the Object Store.

The Object Store provides an alternative to the more traditional locally stored configuration files. In the Object Store an object is a keyed container which aggregates various attributes that refer to the same subject. For example one could have an object to hold the configuration parameters of a given service (or class of services); or perhaps to hold the end-point (and other protocol parameters) where a given service can be contacted.

The object's attributes are: **data**, **indices**, **links**, **annotations**, and **attachments**.

A collection serves no other purpose than to group similar objects together, either based on purpose or type, or based on scope (such as all objects belonging to the same service). Collections can be used without being created first, and there is no option to destroy them (except removing one-by-one all the objects that belong to it). Therefore there are no other implications (in terms of performance or functionality) of placing an object in a collection or another, except perhaps easing operational procedures (such as removing all objects belonging to a service).

The most basic usage of an object would be to store some useful information, and have it available for later access. The stored data can be anything, from JSON or XML to a binary file, and besides the actual data it is characterized by a content-type. Later based on this declared content-type one can decide how to interpret the data. Although there can be a single data item for an object, one could easily use multipart/mixed to bundle together multiple data items; however it is advisable to avoid such a scenario and use either links or attachments.

Access to the data is atomic and concurrent updates are permitted without any locking or conflict resolution mechanisms, the latest update overriding previous ones, thus no isolation with lost-updates being possible. Although the data can be frequently accessed or updated without high overhead, it is advisable to cache operations by using the dedicated HTTP conditional requests. Because the data is stored temporarily in memory, it is advised to keep the amount of data small, well under a 100 kilobytes. Data that is larger should be handled as an attachment. In addition to its data, an object can be augmented with indices which enables efficiently selecting objects on other criteria than just the object key. An object can have multiple indices, each index being characterized by a label and a value, and it is allowed to have multiple indices with the same label.

The major difference between indices presented by this solution and other NoSQL or even SQL databases is that most other solutions build their indices based on the

[1] http://docs.puppetlabs.com/.

[2] http://docs.chef.io/.

actual data. In the case of the object store, the indices are built based on meta-data that is associated with the actual data (the indices attribute). By separating the indexing from the actual data we have greater control over how the data is stored and retrieved. We also optimize for those access patterns where the data changes frequently, but the values used by the indexer stay the same.

Links are the feature which allows an object to reference another one, building in essence a graph. For example one could have a service configuration object, holding specific parameter values, and pointing to a global configuration object, holding default parameter values. A link is characterized by a label and the referenced object key, and it is allowed to have multiple links with the same label or the same referenced object (therefore a many-to-many relation can be created). Unlike indices, links are scoped under the object, are unidirectional, and are not usable in selection criteria. Therefore one can not ascertain which objects reference a given target object (without performing a full scan of the store). The only operation, besides creation and destruction, that can be applied to a link is link-walking, where by starting from an object, one can specify a label and gain access to the referenced object's attributes; link-walking can be applied recursively. Links can be destroyed or created as frequently as necessary as they are not indexed.

Data that logically belongs to the object, but which is either too large to be used as actual data or is static, can be placed within an attachment. Attachments are created in two steps. First, the attachment is created by uploading its content, and obtaining its fingerprint, so if the same data is uploaded twice the fingerprint remains the same thus no extra storage space is consumed. Second, a reference to the attachment (i.e. its fingerprint) is placed within the object with a given label, together with the content-type and size which serves only for informative purposes. The same attachment can be referenced from multiple objects without uploading its data, provided that the fingerprint is known.

Similarly, accessing the attachment of an object is done in two steps: obtaining the attachment reference, then accessing the actual attachment based on its fingerprint. Like with links, attachments are scoped under an object, only their data being globally stored. In terms of efficiency, creating or updating attachments do not have high overhead (except the initial data upload). This is because the various information pertaining to a specific object such as the actual data, meta-data, links, annotations, attachments are not lumped together. These are partitioned, just like vertically partitioned SQL databases. Also, because attachments are identified based on their global qualifier, duplicating or moving an attachments from one object to another doesn't require the re-upload of the entire attachment.

The annotations are meta-data which can be specified for objects or attachments, and are characterized by a label (unique within the same object) and any JSON term as a value. Annotations are those data which if erased do not impact the usage of the object. In general annotations can be used to store ancillary data about the object, especially those used by operational tools. For example, one can specify the creator, tool and possibly the source, ACL's or digital signatures, etc.

The object store has facilities for multi-Cloud deployment via replication. The replication process has three phases: defining on the target (i.e. the server) a replication stream, which yields a token used to authenticate the replication; defining on the initiator (i.e. the client) a matching replication stream; and the actual replication which happens behind the scenes. It must be noted that the replication is one way, namely the target (i.e. the server) continuously streams updates towards the initiator (i.e. the client). If two-way replication is desired, the same process must be followed on both sides.

Regarding conflicts, and because internally the object store exchanges "patches" which only highlight the changes, any conflicting patch is currently ignored. It is therefore highly recommended to confine updates to a certain object only to one of the two replicas. However if multiple changes happen to the same object, and multiple patches are sent, and say the first one yields a conflict, but the rest don't, only the conflicting patch will be discarded, the others being applied. It is possible to obtain replication graphs or trees, including cycles, and the object store handles these properly.

Service Configuration Use Cases

Let us suppose that an operator has several instances of the same service type (i.e. application server or database) which he would like to configure during execution. Moreover the user would like to change the configuration and have it dynamically applied as easily as possible.

Single shared configuration is the most basic scenario. The most simple solution is to store the configuration parameters in an object created before execution is started, preferably JSON term or plain text as the data, or alternatively as an attachment. Then at execution the object's reference is specified as an initialization argument to each of the instantiated services, which retrieve the data and use it to properly configure the service.

If each service continuously polls the object for updates, it can detect when the operator has changed the configuration parameters, and apply the necessary changes (possibly by restarting). This might seem to involve fetching the data over and over again thus incurring large network overhead, such is not necessary true if one uses HTTP conditional requests which is rather efficient.

In the case of **Multiple shared configurations** the services require multiple different configuration parameters grouped in multiple "files", possibly because their syntax is different, or perhaps for better maintenance by the operator. One solution to this problem is to create a master object and using links to point to the other needed configuration objects. As before polling can be applied to detect configuration changes, but because now it involves multiple objects, after an update has been detected a grace period should be used, after which another check should be done, if no other updates have been detected the configurations are applied. This prevents frequently restarting the service while the operator updates sequentially the configuration objects.

8.3.2 Artifact Repository

The artifact repository is designed as archive of artifacts generated in various parts of the MODAClouds Project. The project aims to be able to store information like deployment recipes, maven artifacts, software packages or, basically, any other data. The Artifact repository provides an API for managing the artifacts and for searching the stored data based on their meta-data. The API is REST [1] compliant, and consumable from all MODAClouds components and development tools.

It has to satisfy a set of fairly simple requirements. It has to enable the upload of binary files (BLOB). An artifact may be composed of on or more files under 1 GB. Each artifact has to be versioned as any modification done to an existing artifact has to be identifiable. Also, each file associated with an artifact has to be downloadable and it has to support a number of repositories.

The artifact are stored directly on the file system. The file hierarchy is directly mirrored from the URL structure. This means that the folder structure will include folders for repositories, artifacts, versions and the files. Thus making interrogation extremely intuitive. Another bonus of using a simple file system based approach is the ability to use rsync as the synchronization mechanism between artifact repository deployments. In some ways it can be considered as a stripped down version of the object store. It's main design goal was to create a simple yet powerful mechanism to store software artifact can handle much larger files than the object store.

8.3.3 Load Balancer Controller

The goal of the load balancer controller, is to provide a RESTful API that is able to control and configure Haproxy.[3] For this we used a micro-framework written in python called flask.[4] It is designed as an extensible framework with little dependencies. The main two dependencies are the web server gateway interface subsystem represented by Werkzeug and Jinja2 which provides template support. It is important to note that flask does not natively support some required functionalities such as accessing databases, however there are a significant number of extensions to the framework that resolve these shortcomings [2]. During the project we developed a python Haproxy RESTful API (modaclouds-loadbalancer-controller or MLC) which based on the users input generates a configuration file for the load-balancer (Haproxy) thus controlling its behavior. It exposes both frontend and backend settings as well as limited support for ACL specifications. At this point it is important to note that MLC doesn't check if the ACL triggers are correct when first entered by the operator.

It stores all interactions in a sqlite database, which also serves as the basis of the configuration file. The jinja2 template engine is used to generate the configuration

[3] http://www.haproxy.org/.

[4] http://flask.pocoo.org/docs/0.10/.

file which is then loaded into Haproxy. Currently each configuration file is saved into the database and can be accessed by querying the database. The API is designed to:

- **add, edit and delete resources**—This means that pools, gateways, endpoints and targets can be defined. These represent direct representations of resources present in Haproxy. Each interaction is saved and versioned.
- **set policy**—Load-balancing policies and their associated parameters can be set of each target. For example in the case of round-robin we can set the weights for each target.
- **start Haproxy service**—First a configuration file is generated and used to start the load-balancing service. Each time a new configuration is generated it is reloaded into the already running service.

The MLC is designed to hide as much technical details of Haproxy as possible. This is done in order to make the REST API as agnostic as possible. For example in MLC we use the term gateway to define a frontend server and pool to define the backend servers. This enables easy extension of the MLC and the REST resource structure can be easily mapped onto other load-balancer solutions (such as ngnix) besides Haproxy.

8.3.4 Batch Engine

The main goal of the Batch Engine (BE) is to support the computationally-intensive routines that are to be executed as part of the Filling the Gap Analysis. As there are no tight deadlines, these routines are executed offline, and therefore it is possible to exploit the large datasets of monitoring information collected at runtime. We therefore opt for a BE that exploits a pool of parallel resources. In particular, the BE aims to provide on demand HTC/HPC clusters on top of existing computational Cloud resources (e.g., Eucalyptus, EC2, Flexiant, PTC, etc.).

From a technical perspective, the BE integrates the services provided by the underlying scheduling middleware, particularly the HTCondor workload management system [3]. The BE provides REST API's that allow job execution management (including submission and monitoring).

The API offered by BE is extensible, providing the ability to support new job-scheduling engines or middleware. As the FG analysis techniques were implemented in Matlab, we are making use of the Parallel Toolbox and the APIs offered by the BE to submit and manage the parallel jobs, as well as to retrieve the results. The execution of the FG analysis relies on the Matlab Compiler Runtime (MCR), a free runtime platform to execute standalone applications developed in Matlab.

The main features of the BE are include automatic provisioning using specially-designed Puppet modules, the ability to use existing infrastructure (ex: Amazon EC2, Flexiant) and an API middleware for job control. There are several important features in the BE. First, a REST API (based on JSONRPC2) for controlling the deployment.

This API allows to dynamically specify the architecture of the provisioned cluster, and to reuse predefined models. It allows customizing the cluster based on the required resources (CPU, memory, GPUs, etc.). This API abstracts the cluster deployment operations, including: machine deployment; software provisioning, configuration, monitoring. The API resorts to specially-defined Puppet modules that handle the deployment of all the software components.

It also uses a REST API for job management and monitoring. This REST API abstracts the job management operations and interacts with the back-end HTCondor service. The API provides common operations offered by HTCondor as REST-compliant services. These operations include job submission, data staging, job state notifications, etc.

Lastly a flexible core that allows the addition of various schedulers, each with a different feature set, as required by applications.

From an architectural point of view the BE is composed of four main subsystems: **Batch Engine API**: This subsystem is responsible for interacting with the client applications or users. It handles the requests and delegates them to the other subsystems.

Batch Engine Cluster Manager API: Based on SCT,it uses the Configuration Management subsystem (mainly Puppet) and the Cloud interface for deploying nodes and provisioning the job scheduler (e.g., HTCondor).

Batch Engine Execution Manager: Is responsible with the effective job execution and corresponding event handling (interaction with external components). It dispatches job execution requests to the deployed HTCondor workload manager. The workload manager permits the management of both serial and parallel jobs, feature that will be exploited by applications that use MPI like technologies.

Scheduler: Represents the effective job-scheduling system, responsible for executing the submitted jobs. It also provides the wrapping mechanism needed for offering integration facilities like the job notification API.

Finally, the FG Analyzer calls the Batch Engine periodically and executes several jobs on multiple nodes performing different analyses. For instance, the FG Analyzer can execute several demand estimation procedures in parallel using the Batch Engine to compare the accuracy of them during design time. It also executes the analysis corresponding to different datasets in parallel, thus speeding up the analysis phase.

8.4 Conclusions

As we saw in the previous sections, there are a wide array of tools and platforms that make up the complete MODAClouds solution. The MODAClouds platform core components are comprised of more than 70 RPM packages. Some of these packages are custom repackages of components such as the Java Virtual Machine, Go runtime, python interpreter, Haproxy etc. These are packages on which MODAClouds platform services depend upon. For the sake of completeness we will list the components that comprise each MODAClouds platform:

- **Creator 4Clouds**—Filling the Gap (FG) Analyzier, Functional Modelling Tool, Space 4Cloud, LINE, CloudML, DATA Mapping
- **Venues 4Clouds**—Decision Support System
- **Tower 4Clouds**—Monitoring Manager, DDA, Data Collector, QoS Models, Metrics Observer, Metrics Explorer, Knowledge Base, Matlab SDA, Weka SDA
- **SpaceOps 4Clouds**—Self-Adaptation Stress tester, Load-Balancer reasoner
- **Energizer 4Clouds**—Load Balancing Controller, Object Store, Artifact Repository, Data Migration, mOS image, mOS package builder

Most components from Tower 4Clouds [7], SpaceOps 4Clouds [6] and Energizer4 Clouds [5] are packaged and deployed on top of mOS. Even more significant is the fact that most tools use the supporting services in order to fulfill their function. For example the Load Balancer Reasoner uses the Load Balancer controller supporting service in order to adjust the weights of server backends in Haproxy. Without this REST interface based controller the reasoner would not be able to function. This controller is also used by the Models@Runtime component and can be used by any other application that needs a load balancer. Similarly the object store and artifact repository are used by the Tower 4Clouds components and Load Balancer reasoner, while the Batch engine is used by the Filling the Gap tools.

This chapter has provided an overview of the deployment and architecture of the supporting services and runtime platform. It has highlighted the importance of these types of services which play an important role in the MODAClouds Runtime platform (Energizer 4Cloud). We have also covered how services from Tower 4Clouds and SpaceOps 4Clouds are packaged and later deployed on top of mOS. We have also described the fact that each supporting service is a self contained software package meaning that they can be easily reused and modified. The four supporting services, Object Store, Artifact Repository, Load-Balancer Controller and Batch Engine have been described and rationale behind their design has been covered. Lastly these services are put into context of the MODAClouds runtime platform (with details how each supporting service is integrated into sub-system of the runtime platform).

References

1. Fielding RT, Taylor RN (2002) Principled design of the modern web architecture. ACM Trans Internet Technol 2(2) ISSN 1533-5399
2. Grinberg M (2014) Flask web development: developing web applications with python. O'Reilly Media Inc. ISBN 1449372627
3. Thain D, Tannenbaum T, Livny M (2005) Distributed computing in practice: the condor experience. Concurr Pract Exp 17
4. Petcu D, Macariu G, Panica S, Crăciun (2013) Portable cloud applications—from theory to practice. Future Gener Comput Syst 29. ISSN 0167-739X
5. Iuhasz G, Panica S, Casale G, Wang W, Jamshidi P, Ardagna D, Ciavotta M, Whigham D, Ferry N, González R (2015) MODAClouds D6.5.3—runtime environment final release. http://www.modaclouds.eu

6. Fortiş F, Iuhasz G, Neagul M, Casale G, Perez J, Wang W (2015) MODAClouds D5.3.2—techniques for filling the gap between design time and runtime. http://www.modaclouds.eu
7. Casale G, Weikun W, Miglierina M, Munteanu V (2014) MODAClouds D6.3.2—monitoring platform final release. http://www.modaclouds.eu

Chapter 9
Models@Runtime for Continuous Design and Deployment

Nicolas Ferry and Arnor Solberg

9.1 Introduction

Nowadays, software systems are leveraging upon an aggregation of dedicated infrastructures and platforms, which leads to the design of large scale, distributed, and dynamic systems. The need to evolve and update such systems after delivery is often inevitable, for example, due to changes in the requirements, maintenance, or needs for advancing the quality of services such as scalability and performances. The demands to evolve and update the systems typically increase with Cloud-based systems, since the Cloud enable to dynamically adjust and evolve the platforms and infrastructures, while previously these were very much rigid and more or less fixed. This implies on the one hand more opportunities and flexibility to better evolve and adjust the systems to various needs and requirements, on the other hand the complexity of designing, delivering, managing and maintaining such systems challenges current software engineering techniques.

As stated in [1], in order to reduce delivery time and fostering continuous evolution of these systems, there is a need to close the gap between development and operation activities. However, developers and operators are often working in separate teams with specific roles, and thus, prefer to use the specific languages they feel comfortable with. This hinders the knowledge sharing between these teams, thereby, on the one hand making it difficult for designers to obtain and understand feedback on the status of the operated system that could be useful to evolve it, and on the other hand making it difficult for operators to analyse and comment on the impact of proposed or implemented design changes. As promoted by the DevOps movement [2]. This issue can be better handled by facilitating collaboration between developers and

N. Ferry · A. Solberg (✉)
Stiftelsen SINTEF, Postboks 4760 Sluppen, 7465 Trondheim, Norway
e-mail: Arnor.Solberg@sintef.no

N. Ferry
e-mail: Nicolas.Ferry@sintef.no

E. Di Nitto et al. (eds.), *Model-Driven Development and Operation of Multi-Cloud Applications*, PoliMI SpringerBriefs,
DOI 10.1007/978-3-319-46031-4_9

operators for example through aligning concepts and languages used in development and operation, and supporting them with automated tools that help reducing the gap and improving the flexibility and efficiency of the delivery life-cycle (e.g., resource provisioning and deployment).

In particular, continuous integration [3] tools play a key role, for example, through the significant increase of the frequency of integration it ensures immediate feedback to developers. Continuous integration also enable frequent releases, more control in terms of predictability (as opposed to integration surprises in less frequent and more heavy integration cycles) as well as productivity and communication. Continuous deployment can be seen as a part of the continuous integration practice and is defined as: "*Continuous deployment is the practice of continuously deploying good software builds automatically to some environment, but not necessarily to actual users*" [3].

In the context of Cloud applications and multi-Cloud applications [4] (i.e., applications that can be deployed across multiple Cloud infrastructures and platforms), designers and operators typically seek to exploit the peculiarities of the many existing Cloud solutions and to optimise performance, availability, and cost. In such context, there is a pressing need for tools supporting automated and continuous deployment to reduce time-to-market but also to facilitate testing and validation of the design choices. However, current approaches are not sufficient to properly manage the complexity of the development and administration of multi-Cloud systems [5].

In this chapter we present the mechanism and tooling within the MODAClouds approach to reduce the gap between developers and operators by supporting continuous deployment of multi-Cloud applications. In order to reduce the gap between developers and operators we apply the same concepts and language for deployment and resource provisioning at development time and at operation time (the CLOUDMLpresented in Chap. 3). To automate the continous deployment and resource provisioning we have developed a deployment and resource provisioning engine based on the principles of the Models@Runtime approach [6]. This engine is responsible for enacting the continuous deployment of multi-Cloud applications as well as the dynamic adaptation of their deployment and resource provisioning including operations such as scaling out and bursting of parts of an application. The engine "speaks" the language of CLOUDML, thus, it provides the same concepts and abstractions for the operators as applied by the developers.

The remainder of the paper is organised as follows. Section 9.2 presents our model-based approach. Section 9.3 provides an overview of the MODAClouds Models@Runtime engine. Sections 9.3.1 and 9.3.2 details how the engine can be used to continuously adapt the deployment of an application in a declarative and imperative way, respectively. Section 9.3.3 presents the mechanism to monitor the status of the running system. Section 9.3.4 details the mechanisms enabling remote interaction with the engine. Finally, Sect. 9.4 presents some related work and Sect. 9.5 draws some conclusions.

9.2 The Models@Runtime Approach

Model-Driven Engineering (MDE) techniques have shown to be effective in supporting design activities [7]. MDE is a branch of software engineering which aims at improving the productivity, quality and cost-effectiveness of software development by shifting the paradigm from code-centric to model-centric. Models and modelling languages, as the main artefacts of the development process, enable developers to work at a higher level of abstraction rather than at the level of implementation details. However, as stated in [6], applying the classical MDE approach for software evolution would be impractical. Indeed, this would typically result in generating the new solution, stopping the running system before replacing it by the new one, this in contrast with common expectations for Cloud services to have more or less 100 % up-time. In order to address this issue, the Models@Runtime approach has emerged.

Models@Runtime [6, 8] is an architectural pattern for dynamic adaptive systems that leverage models as executable artefacts supporting the execution of the system. This way, Models@Runtime promotes the DevOps method, by providing a unique model-based representation of the applications for both design- and run-time activities (i.e., for developers and operators). As depicted in Fig. 9.1, Models@Runtime provides an abstract representation of the underlying running system, which facilitates reasoning, simulation, and enactment of adaptation actions. A change in the running system is automatically reflected in the model of the current system. Similarly, a modification to this model is enacted on the running system on demand. This causal connection enables the continuous evolution of the system with no strict boundaries between design-time and run-time activities.

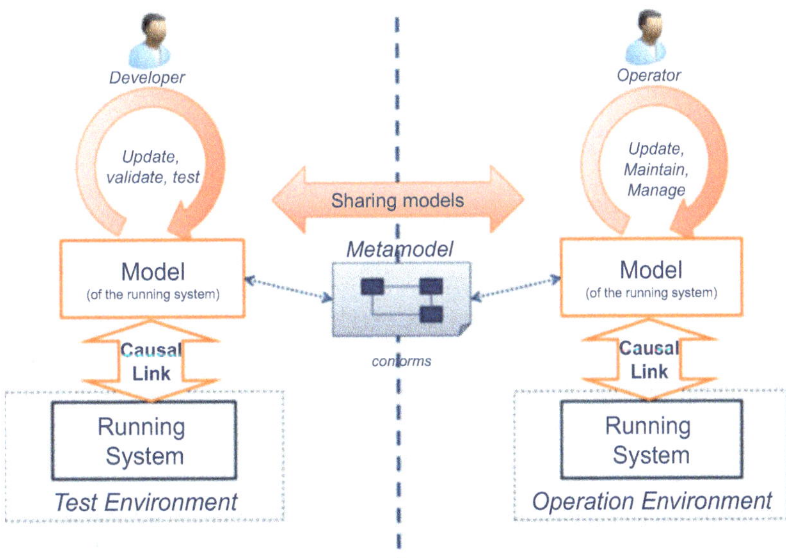

Fig. 9.1 Continuous deployment using Models@Runtime

Exploiting Models@Runtime for the continuous deployment of Cloud-based applications would thus result in the process depicted in Fig. 9.1. A developer team can specify a model of the deployment of its application (typically exploiting a domain-specific language such as CLOUDML) and thus automatically enact this deployment into a test environment. The team can therefore benefit from this test environment to tune its development and redeploy it automatically. Any change made to the deployment model will be enacted on demand on the running system whilst its status will be reflected in the model providing useful feedback. Once the new release is validated, it can be provided together with the associated deployment model to the operation team. The latter can in turn exploit the model to deploy the new release in a production environment. The operators can thus tune this model to maintain and manage the running system. Because the models shared by the developers and operators conform to the same metamodel, at any time they can share and exchange information.

9.3 The MODAClouds Models@Runtime Engine

The MODAClouds Models@Runtime environment relies on the Cloud Modelling Language [9] (CLOUDML) in order to provide a deployment model causally connected to the running system. As a result, the Models@Runtime maintains deployment models at two levels of abstraction: Cloud provider-independent models (CPIM) and Cloud provider-specific models (CPSM) as advocated by MODA-CloudML. On the one hand, any modification to the CPIM will be reflected in the CPSM and, in turn, propagated on-demand onto the running system. On the other hand, any change in the running system will be reflected in the CPSM, which, in turn, can be assessed with respect to the CPIM. This way, by exploiting the MODA-CloudML deployment model, the Models@Runtime environment seamlessly bridges the gap between the runtime and design-time activities. Figure 9.2 shows the CPSM of the Constellation case study (see Chap. 13) defined using the MODAClouds IDE and managed by the Models@Runtime engine.

Figure 9.3 depicts the architecture of the MODAClouds Models@Runtime engine. A reasoning system can read the current CPSM (step 1), which describes the actual running system, and produces a target CPSM (step 2). Then, the runtime environment calculates the difference between the current CPSM and the target CPSM (step 3). Finally, the adaptation engine enacts the adaptation modifying only the parts of the system necessary to account for the difference, and the target CPSM becomes the current CPSM (step 4). For each modification of the running system, the synchronization engine propagate notifications describing the change to third party entities.

Once the application is deployed, the Models@Runtime engine interacts with the Cloud providers API in order to observe the status of the Cloud services used. This mechanism is based on a pulling approach for which the frequency of the requests to the providers API can be parameterized.

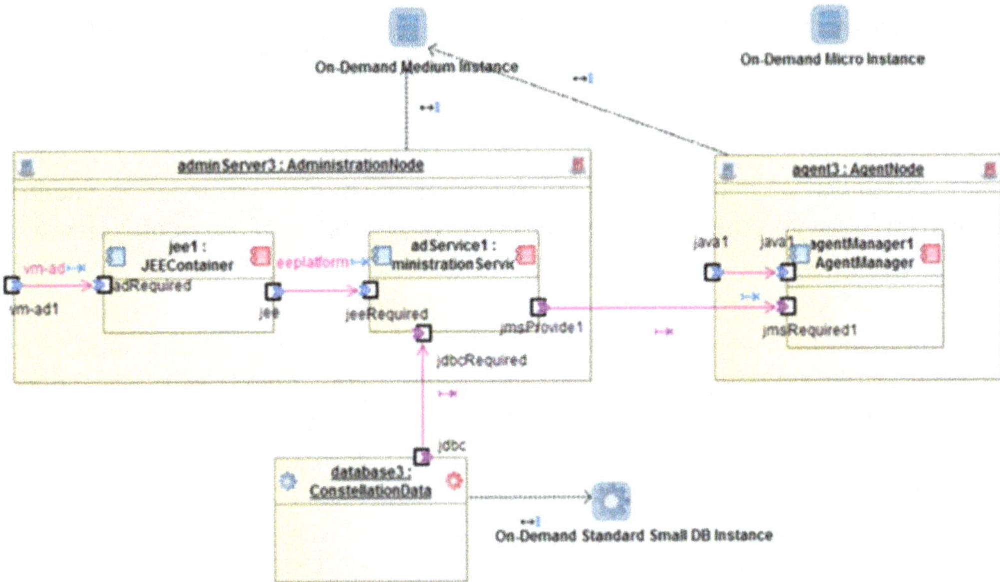

Fig. 9.2 CPSM of the Constellation case study

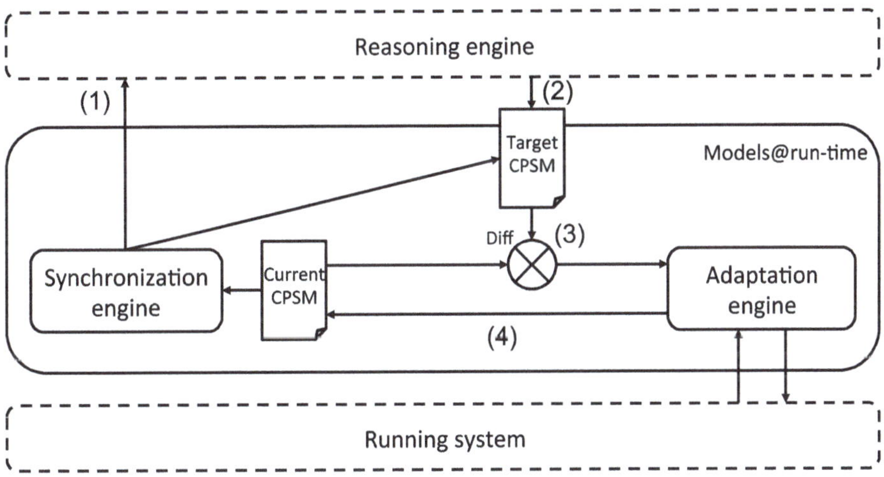

Fig. 9.3 The CloudML Models@Runtime architecture

Using the Models@Runtime engine, the deployment of an application can be adapted in both imperative and declarative ways. The imperative approach requires the explicit definition through a set of predefined instructions of how to reach the desired deployment. In contrast, the declarative approach requires the specification of the desired deployment and then the plan on how to reach that deployment is derived automatically. Both approaches result in a target CPSM that is consumed by a comparison engine, which computes the difference between the target model and the model of the running system. The result of this process is thus exploited to manipulate and adapt only the parts of the system necessary to account for the difference. In the following subsections we detail first the comparison engine and then the main adaptation commands.

9.3.1 The Comparison Engine

The inputs to the `Comparison engine` (also called `Diff`) are the current and target deployment models. The output is a list of actions representing the required changes to transform the current model into the target model. The types of potential actions are listed in Table 9.1 and result in: (i) modification of the deployment and resource provisioning topology, (ii) modifications of the components' properties, or (iii) modifications of their status on the basis of their life-cycle. In particular, the status of an external component (i.e., representing a VM or a PaaS solution) can be: `running`, `stopped` or in `error`, whilst the status of an internal component (i.e., representing the software to be deployed on an enternal component) can be: `uninstalled`, `installed`, `configured`, `running` or in `error`.

The comparison engine processes the entities composing the deployment models in the following order: `external components`, `internal components`, `execution binding`, to `relationships`, on the basis of the logical dependencies between these concepts. In this way, all the components required by another component are deployed first. For each of these concepts, the engine compare the two sets of instances from the current and target models. This comparison is achieved

Table 9.1 Types of output actions generated by the `Comparison engine`

Action	Parameter	Effect
addExternalComponent	ExternalComponent	Provision a new virtual machine or prepare a PaaS service
removeExternalComponent	ExternalComponent	Terminate a virtual machine or stop a PaaS service
addInternalComponent	InternalComponent	Deploy the internal component on the target virtual machine
removeInternalComponent	InternalComponent	Remove the internal component instance from its current host
addCommunication	Communication	Configure the endpoints of the communication
removeCommunication	Communication	Disconnect the endpoints of the communication
addHosting	Hosting	Configure the endpoints of the hosting
removeHosting	Hosting	Disconnect the endpoints of the hosting
setStatus	Status	Change the status of a component
setProperty	Property	Change a property of a component

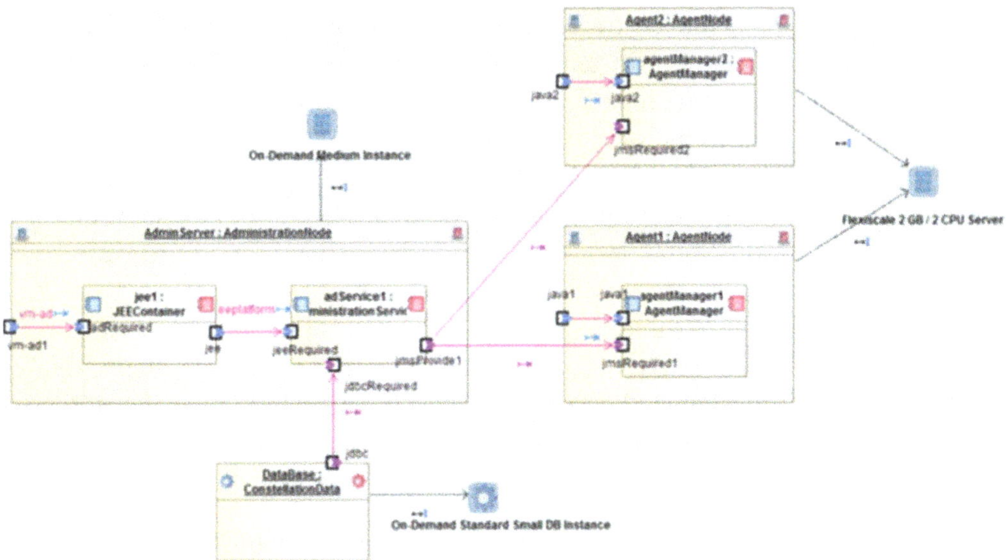

Fig. 9.4 An example of target CPSM of the Constellation case study

on the matching of both the properties of the instances and their types as well as on the basis of their dependencies (e.g., if the host of a component has changed the component might be redeployed). For each unmatched instance from the current model a `remove` action with the instance as argument is created. Similarly, for each unmatched instance from the target model an `add` action with the instance as argument is generated.

As an example, the comparison between the models depicted in Figs. 9.2 and 9.4 results in the following modifications in the deployment of the Constellation server: a new VM is provisioned on Flexiscale, Agent 1 is migrated from the on-demand medium instance to the new VM, and finally a new Agent is also installed on the same VM.

We always give a higher priority to the target model, which for example means that any virtual machine instance in the target model that does exist in the current model will be regarded as one that need to be created. Conversely, any virtual machine in the current model that does not exist in the target model will be removed. Coping with changes that happens during reasoning could be handled in various ways, for instance as part of a third step of the adaptation process (model checking). Currently, the Models@Runtime engine does not handle changes that might occur during the time of reasoning.

9.3.2 *Adaptation Commands*

As stated before, the deployment of an application can be dynamically adapted by exploiting the set of commands exposed by the engine. In particular, within the MODAClouds runtime environment, the Models@Runtime engine is responsible for enacting adaptation actions such as the scaling and bursting of an application.

These actions can be achieved by directly providing a deployment model to the Models@Runtime engine. For instance, the simplest way to perform a bursting at the IaaS level consists in updating the model of the running system by either updating the provider associated to the type of the VM instance or by simply changing the type of a VM instance with one associated to the desired provider. This approach allows fine grained tuning of the deployment of an application to the needs of new contexts or requirements, however, it can be a complex task for a third party to be responsible for evolving to the new deployment model.

Therefore, the Models@Runtime engine also provides high level commands that avoid direct manipulation of the models. In particular, the `scale` command enable scaling out a VM in the same Cloud and the `burst` command enable scaling out a VM in another Cloud. Currently, in both these cases the first task of the engine consists in modifying the current deployment model as follow:

1. Create a new instance of VM with unique name and port names of the same type as the VM to be scaled. In case of bursting, the provider associated to the new instance is the one specified in the bursting command.
2. For each internal component instance running on the VM to be scaled, create an instance of the same type and add an execution binding between each of them and the newly created VM. All new instances are created with unique names and port names.
3. Identify all the relationship instances involving the internal component running on the VM to be scaled and for each of them, create an instance of the same type with unique names. The endpoints of these new relationship instances are: the newly created internal component instance and the same component as the one involved in the original relationship.

Once the deployment model is updated, the engine acts differently depending of the type of command. In case of bursting to a new provider, the engine simply exploit the Models@Runtime comparison mechanism and trigger a classical deployment, whilst in the case of scaling within the same Cloud it operates as follows:

1. If not existing, create an image of the VM to be scaled.
2. Provision a VM using this image.
3. Reconfigure all components on the basis of the newly created relationship.
4. Restart the new components.

In case a set of VM instances cannot be further scaled (e.g., in case there are no more resources available on a private Cloud), the Models@Runtime engine acts as follows: The target model generated by the scale out command is considered as the current model of the system and the status of the newly created VM is set to `error` whilst the status of its hosted internal components is set to `unrecognized`.

In order to reduce the time needed to scale a VM, another provided feature is to provision VMs in advance with all the required software component deployed on it, and thus making them ready to be started or stopped on demand. In order to support such an approach, the Models@Runtime engine offers commands to start and stop components. These commands can be applied to both external and internal components. In the case of external components, this is achieved by exploiting the various Cloud provider APIs, whilst in the case of internal components it consists in calling the start and stop commands of the resources associated to the component. In both cases, the components have to be provisioned and installed upfront.

9.3.3 State Tracking

The Models@Runtime engine allows tracking the status of a deployment or adaptation as well as the status of Cloud resources once a multi-Cloud application is deployed. In order to track the state of Cloud resources, a simple monitoring agent is started in a parallel thread. Modules (one for each provider) can then be attached to the agent which are then responsible for interacting with the providers API in order to monitor the status of the Cloud resources being used. The frequency at which these status checks are performed can be configured manually or programmatically. Once performed and in case the status of a Cloud resource has changed, the agent exploits the Models@Runtime synchronization mechanism in order to reflect this change into the CPSM of the running system. As a result, all the registered clients of the Models@Runtime engine are notified of the update. Similarly, the status of the internal component is changed during the deployment process depending on the result of each deployment command.

The Models@Runtime engine is also synchronized with the MODAClouds monitoring platform (see Chap. 5) so that it can subscribe to receive some of the metrics collected by the monitoring platform.

In addition, this synchronization enable the co-evolution of the monitoring platform with the Cloud-application (e.g., when a service bursts from one provider to another, the monitoring activity has to be adapted accordingly). By synchronizing the Models@Runtime engine and the monitoring platform, the latter can dynamically and automatically be adapted to best fit with the actual deployment of the application.

In case the deployment of an application is adapted, the Models@Runtime engine, can communicate the changes to the monitoring platform and update the deployment of the data collectors. The monitoring platform can in turn adapt its own configuration accordingly, exploiting the Monitoring Manager which is the main coordinator of the monitoring activity. It manages and configures all the monitoring components including the model used by the Data Collectors (DCs) so that the retrieving of data can be adapted accordingly.

The deployment or un-deployment of Data Collectors can be done for example, to free resources, to replace a Data Collector with a new one that may offer slightly some different features, or when a monitored component is migrated. In addition, when the deployment of the running system is modified (e.g., bursting or migration from one provider to another), the monitoring activity will restart on the new machine using the same settings and rules used on the old one. Since the Models@Runtime engine can manage multi-Cloud applications and because the DCs are provider-agnostic, the migration can be performed from one provider to another.

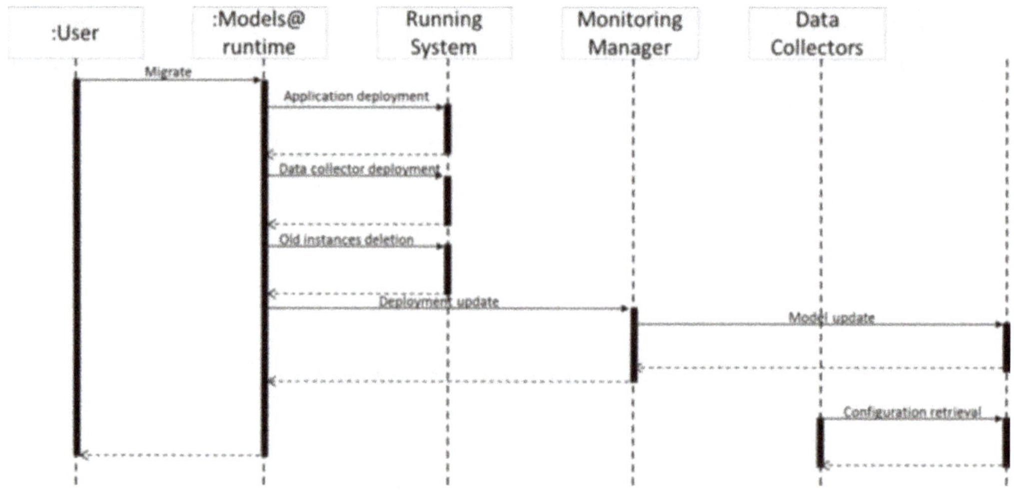

Fig. 9.5 Adaptation of the monitoring platform during the bursting process

Figure 9.5 details the interactions between the reasoning engine, the monitoring platform and the Models@Runtime engine during the migration of an application.

First, the Models@Runtime engine instantiates a new machine and deploys the application on it. Then it deploys the Data Collectors on the VM and finally removes the old instantiation of the application. At this stage, the Models@Runtime engine notifies to the Monitoring Manager the changes in the deployment (e.g., status of the new machine, address of the Data Collector), and the Monitoring Manager uses these information to autonomously update the KB from which the Data Collector retrieve its own configuration.

The communication from the model@runtime engine to the monitoring platform is performed through the REST APIs offered by the Monitoring Manager which is the main coordinator of the monitoring activity.

9.3.4 Interaction with the Models@Runtime Engine

The Models@Runtime environment also provides synchronisation mechanisms for remote third-party entities (e.g., such as the MODAClouds reasoning engines) to adapt the system. This synchronisation is implemented by the propagation of changes in both directions, namely `notification` and `command`. A notification allows the Models@Runtime engine to propagate its change to third-parties, whilst a command enables modifications on the current CPSM. This mechanism is exploited by various MODAClouds runtime components such as the MODAClouds reasoning engine to be informed of the changes occurring in the deployment of the running system and then adapt it accordingly. Because the two models used by two players can be isolated from each other and might not be aware of the whole model state, only the sequence of modifications is propagated, without carrying the start state of each change. Therefore, either notification or command is a sequence of modifications.

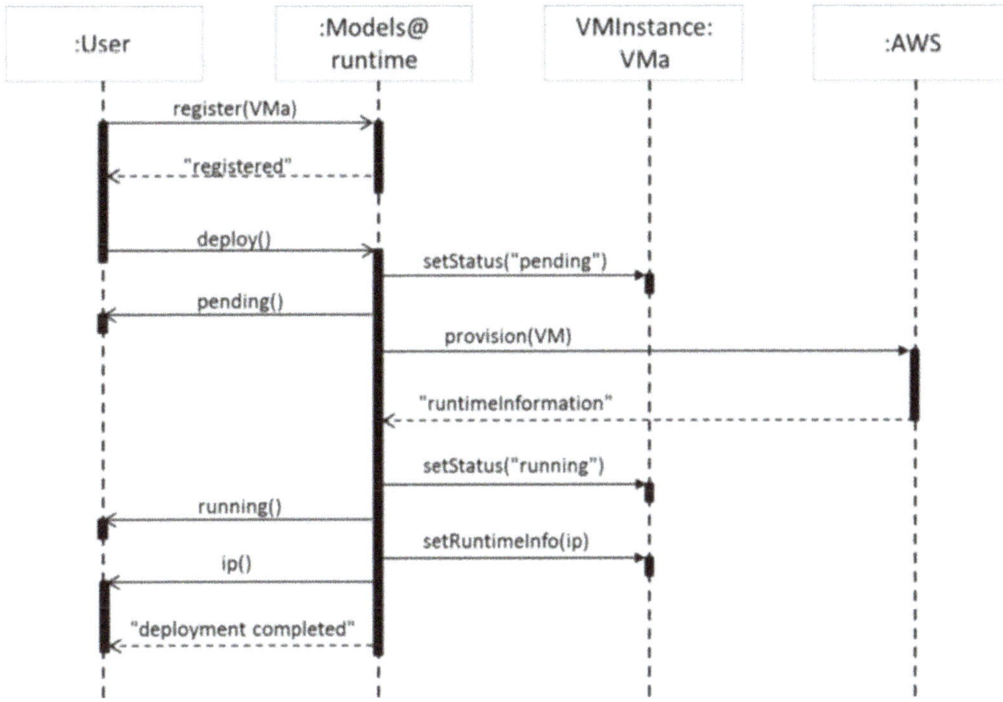

Fig. 9.6 Models@Runtime notification mechanism

Figure 9.6 presents a typical usage of the notification mechanism. First a client use an asynchronous command to register for being notified when a change occur on a specific VM. Then she exploits another asynchronous command to initiate a deployment. As a result, the Models@Runtime engine (i) changes the status of the object in the model that represents this VM to `pending` and sends a message that depicts this change to the client, and (ii) initiates the actual provisioning of the VM. Once terminated, the status of the VM is changed to `running` and the corresponding notification is sent. In addition, the Models@Runtime engine retrieves from the provider and populate the model with a set of runtime information such as the IP of the VM. For each of these changes in the model a notification is sent.

Currently, the communication with third-parties is achieved using the WebSocket protocol[1] in order to enable light-weight communications. Events are encoded as plain text and we provide a domain-specific language to define them, including the text format, the query and criteria to locate the relevant model element, the modification or change on the element, and the combination of other events. We defined the standard MOF (Meta-Object Facility) reflection modifications as the primitive events, and allow developers to further define higher level events as the composition of primitive ones. Using this language, one can also define the model changes on an abstract model as the composition of events on a concrete model, and

[1] http://www.websocket.org/.

in this way, it can be used as an event-based transformation. After each adaptation, the engine wraps the modification events into one message and send it to the WebSocket port.

In order to handle concurrency (i.e., adaptation actions coming from several third-parties), the Models@Runtime uses a simple transaction-based mechanism. The WebSocket component creates a single transaction which contains all the modifications from a third-party, and passes it to a concurrency handler. The handler queues the transactions, and executes them one after another without overlapping. Since all the modifications are simply assignments or object instantiation commands on the model in the form of Java objects, the time to finish a transaction of events is significantly shorter than the adaptation process.

9.4 Related Work

In the Cloud community, several solutions support the deployment, management and adaptation of Cloud-based application. However, to the best of our knowledge, none of them provides the same concepts and abstractions at runtime for the operators as applied by the developers.

Advanced frameworks such as Cloudify,[2] Puppet[3] or Chef[4] provide capabilities for the automatic provisioning, deployment, monitoring, and adaptation of Cloud systems without being language-dependent. Such solutions provide DSL to capture and enact Cloud-based system management. The Topology and Orchestration Specification for Cloud Applications (TOSCA) [10] standard is a specification developed by the OASIS. TOSCA provides a language for specifying the components comprising the topology of Cloud applications along with the processes for their orchestration.

In addition, several approaches focus on the management of application based on PaaS solutions. Sellami et al. [11] propose an model-driven approach for PaaS-independent provisioning and management of Cloud applications. This approach includes a way to model the PaaS application to be deployed as well as a REST API to provision and manage the described application. The Cloud4SOA EU project [12] provides a framework for facilitating the matchmaking, management, monitoring and migration of application on PaaS platforms.

By constrast with the Models@Runtime engine, in all these approaches, the resulting models are not causally connected to the running system, and may become irrelevant as maintenance operations are carried out. The approaches proposed in the CloudScale [13] and Reservoir [14] projects suffer similar limitations.

---

[2] http://www.cloudifysource.org/.

[3] https://puppetlabs.com/.

[4] http://www.opscode.com/chef/.

On the other hand, the work of Shao et al. [15] was a first attempt to build a models@runtime platform for the cloud, but remains restricted to monitoring, without providing support for configuration enactment. To the best of our knowledge, the CLOUDMLModels@Runtime engine is thus the first attempt to reconcile cloud management solutions with modelling practices through the use of models@run-time.

9.5 Conclusion

In this chapter we presented how the MODAClouds Models@Runtime approach leverage upon MDE techniques and methods at runtime to support the continuous design and deployment of multi-Cloud applications. This includes support for their dynamic provisioning, deployment and adaptation by third party entities. Thanks to the proposed approach it is possible to exploit the same concepts and language for deployment and resource provisioning at both development and operation time. This facilitates interaction between developer and operation teams and helps reducing the gap between the two related activities as advocated by the DevOps movement.

References

1. Httermann M (2012) DevOps for developers. Apress
2. Humble J, Farley D (2010) Continuous delivery: reliable software releases through build, test, and deployment automation. Addison-Wesley Professional
3. Fitzgerald B, Stol KJ (2014) Continuous software engineering and beyond: trends and challenges. In: Proceedings of the 1st international workshop on rapid continuous software engineering. ACM, pp 1–9
4. Petcu D (2014) Consuming resources and services from multiple clouds. J Grid Comput 1–25
5. Ardagna D, Di Nitto E, Casale G, Petcu D, Mohagheghi P, Mosser S, Matthews P, Gericke A, Balligny C, D'Andria F, Nechifor CS, Sheridan C (2012) MODACLOUDS, a model-driven approach for the design and execution of applications on multiple clouds. In: ICSE MiSE: international workshop on modelling in software engineering. IEEE/ACM, pp 50–56
6. Blair G, Bencomo N, France R (2009) Models@run.time. IEEE Comput 42(10):22–27
7. Ruscio DD, Paige RF, Pierantonio A (eds) Special issue on success stories in model driven engineering 89(Part B) Elsevier (2014)
8. Morin B, Barais O, Jézéquel JM, Fleurey F, Solberg A (2009) Models@Run.time to support dynamic adaptation. IEEE Comput 42(10):44–51
9. Ferry N, Song H, Rossini A, Chauvel F, Solberg A (2014) CloudMF: applying MDE to tame the complexity of managing multi-cloud applications. In: Proceedings of UCC 2014: 7th IEEE/ACM international conference on utility and cloud computing
10. Palma D, Spatzier T (2013) Topology and orchestration specification for cloud applications (TOSCA). Technical report, Organization for the Advancement of Structured Information Standards (OASIS)
11. Sellami M, Yangui S, Mohamed M, Tata S (2013) PaaS-independent provisioning and management of applications in the cloud. In O'Conner L (ed) CLOUD 2013: 6th IEEE international conference on cloud computing. IEEE Computer Society, pp 693–700
12. Cloud4SOA EU project. http://www.cloud4soa.com

13. Brataas G, Stav E, Lehrig S, Becker S, Kopčak G, Huljenic D (2013) CloudScale: scalability management for cloud systems. In: ICPE 2013: 4th ACM/SPEC international conference on performance engineering. ACM, pp 335–338
14. Rochwerger B, Breitgand D, Levy E, Galis A, Nagin K, Llorente IM, Montero R, Wolfsthal Y, Elmroth E, Cáceres J, Ben-Yehuda M, Emmerich W, Galán F (2009) The reservoir model and architecture for open federated cloud computing. IBM J Res Dev 53(4):535–545
15. Shao J, Wei H, Wang Q, Mei H (2010) A runtime model based monitoring approach for cloud. In: CLOUD 2010: 3rd IEEE international conference on cloud computing. IEEE Computer Society, pp 313–320

Chapter 10
Closing the Loop Between Ops and Dev

Weikun Wang, Giuliano Casale and Gabriel Iuhasz

10.1 Introduction

DevOps [1] is a recent trend in software engineering that bridges the gap between software development and operations, putting the developer in greater control of the operational environment in which the application runs. To support Quality-of-Service (QoS) analysis, the developer may rely on software performance models. However, to provide reliable estimates, the input parameters must be continuously updated and accurately estimated. Accurate estimation is challenging because some parameters are not explicitly tracked by log files requiring deep monitoring instrumentation that poses large overheads, unacceptable in production environments.

The MODAClouds Filling-the-Gap (FG) tool is a component for parametrization of performance models designed in MODAClouds continuously at run time. The FG tool implements a set of statistical estimation algorithms to parameterize performance models from runtime monitoring data. Multiple algorithms are included, allowing for alternative ways to obtain estimates for different metrics, but with an emphasis on resource demand estimation. A distinguishing feature of FG tool is that it supports advanced algorithms to estimate parameters based on response times and queue-length data, which makes the tool useful in particular for applications running

W. Wang · G. Casale (✉)
Department of Computing, Imperial College London, 180 Queens Gate,
London SW7 2AZ, UK
e-mail: g.casale@imperial.ac.uk

W. Wang
e-mail: weikun.wang11@imperial.ac.uk

G. Iuhasz
Institute E-Austria Timişoara, West University of Timişoara, B-dul Vasile Pârvan 4,
300223 Timişoara, Romania
e-mail: iuhasz.gabriel@info.uvt.ro

E. Di Nitto et al. (eds.), *Model-Driven Development and Operation of Multi-Cloud Applications*, PoliMI SpringerBriefs,
DOI 10.1007/978-3-319-46031-4_10

in virtualized environments where utilization readings are not always available. In addition, the FG tool offers support for parallel computations, integrates monitoring data acquisition, and generates performance reports.

10.2 FG Architecture

The FG tool is consisted of four sub-components: the Local DB, the FG Analyzer, the FG Reporter and the FG Actuator. Figure 10.1 descries the relation between each component.

We show here a brief introduction of each component:

- The Local DB is a local database, which is built upon the Fuseki[1] database. The Local DB is in charge of periodically obtaining runtime monitoring data that will be used by the FG Analyzer from the Monitoring History DB. Due to the nature of Fuseki database, the monitoring data will be stored in RDF format in the local DB.
- The FG Analyzer is the main component of the FG and will be described in Sect. 10.2.1. After receiving runtime data stored in the Local DB, the FG Analyzer provides accurate estimates to parametrise the design-time Quality-of-Service (QoS) models developed in MODAClouds. These parameters include the resource demand, the think time and the total number of jobs running in the system.
- The FG Reporter, illustrated in Sect. 10.2.3, periodically generates reports on the application behavior at run time. The reports shows the performance of the application by presenting performance metrics such as the response time and the throughput of the jobs.
- The FG Actuator (see Sect. 10.2.2) is responsible for updating the IDE models and the QoS models based on the result from the FG Analyzer.

10.2.1 FG Analyzer

One of the ultimate objectives of the Filling the Gap (FG) component is to provide accurate estimates to the parameters in the design-time QoS models. These QoS models are key in the what-if analysis performed at design time, and in the decision of the optimal resource provisioning for the Cloud application. These models are initially parameterised using expert-knowledge or data collected in small deployments. Once the application has been deployed on the Cloud, possibly in a production environment, the FG analysis is deployed to obtain estimates based on monitoring data collected at run time.

[1] http://jena.apache.org/documentation/serving_data/.

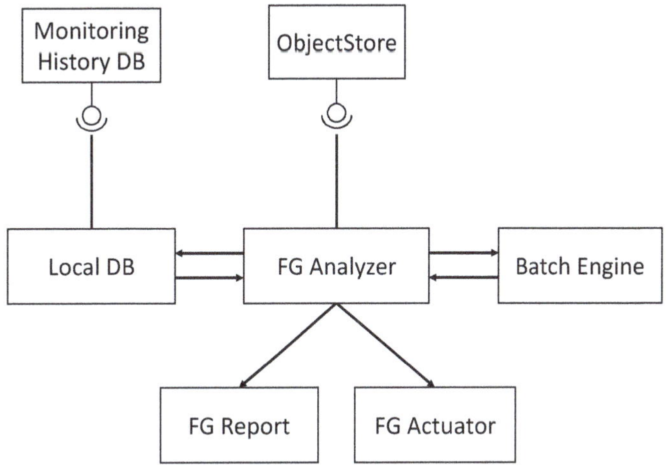

Fig. 10.1 FG architecture

The QoS models developed in MODAClouds are based on layered queueing network models, which capture the contention between users for the available hardware and software resources, and the interaction between them. In particular, we make use of closed models that are well-suited for software systems, as real applications are layered, and the interactions between layers are typically due to admission control or finite threading limits [2]. To parameterise these models, it is essential to estimate the inter-request times, modeled as think times, as well as the resource consumption exerted by each request. Inter-request times can be extracted from the information and the data that is typically tracked by application- or container-level logs. As to the gathering of the run time configuration, the FG Analyzer obtains the configuration file from the Object Store which is kept by the QoS engineer.

Resource consumptions, also referred to as demands, are however harder to obtain as this is not tracked by logs, and the deep monitoring instrumentations typically required pose unacceptably large overheads, especially at high resolutions. Since requests typically complete in a few milliseconds, individual monitoring becomes cost-expensive to perform in a production system. To address this problem, our approach is to take coarse-grained measurements and apply statistical inference to estimate mean resource demands. Most of existing mean demand estimation approaches rely on the regression against utilization data [3–13], however, utilization measurements are not always available, for instance in Platform-as-a-Service (PaaS) deployments where the resource layer is hidden to the application and thus protected from external monitoring.

In the FG Analyzers, two demand estimation algorithms, **GQL** (Gibbs sampling method with Queue Length data) and **MINPS**, have been proposed as an original contribution within the MODAClouds research [14]. The fact that utilization measurements are not required makes these methods suitable for applications deployed on both IaaS and PaaS. In addition to these two methods, the FG Analysis component implements existing demand estimation methods. In particular, the component supports the methods implemented for the Statistical Data Analyzers (SDA) in the Monitoring Platform.

Since the methods supported by the FG Analysis are computationally efficient, large sample set can be utilized for the analysis. The FG component thus supports the following three demand estimation methods: the utilization-based optimization (UBO) method from [15], the utilization-based regression (UBR) method from [12], and the Extended RPS method from [16]. A short description of these methods is provided in Sect. 10.4.

Finally, the FG Analyzer calls the Batch Engine periodically and executes several jobs on multiple nodes performing different analyses. For instance, the FG Analyzer can execute several demand estimation procedures in parallel using the Batch Engine to compare the accuracy of them during design time. It also executes the analysis corresponding to different datasets in parallel, thus speeding up the analysis phase.

10.2.2 FG Actuator

In order to improve the accuracy of the design-time QoS models developed in WP5, the FG tool estimates the parameters of the models with the monitoring information collected at runtime. Then the task of updating the actual model is fulfilled by FG Actuator, which updates the resource demand, think time, number of users circulating in the system in both the QoS models and PCM models given the input from the FG Analyzer.

Since the QoS models and PCM models may have inconsistent names for the deployed resources, the FG actuator requires a properties file indicating the mapping of the resource names between the two models. In addition, the name of the job classes could be different from the data analyzers and the models. A job class mapping file should also be provided.

Given the path to the model files, the FG Actuator first updates the resource demands in the QoS models by matching the resource and job class names. Then it obtains an id for the particular resource and class of job. This id is identical to the one defined in the PCM model. Therefore the FG Actuator uses this id to update the resource demand in the PCM model. Updating the think time and number of jobs in the system is straightforward by just changing the corresponding fields in the XML file.

10.2.3 FG Reporter

In order to provide the developer with runtime information of the application behavior at runtime, the FG periodically generates a report. The report is a PDF document containing tables and figures of performance metrics such as response time, resource demands and throughput, which helps the developer to identify periods of high and low load, as well as to understand the application behavior under the different scenarios.

The automatically report generation relies on the DynamicReports,[2] which is an open-source library based on JasperReports[3] for generating reports based on complex datasets. The DynamicReports supports a wide range of data formats, including relational databases, XML, XLS, and CVS files, among others. In particular, we utilized its ability to integrate JSON (JavaScript Object Notation) format, as this format is expressive and easily understandable.

The FG Reporter periodically receives JSON files generated from the FG Analyzer, which contains necessary information regarding the application such as the think time, response time, resource demands, etc. Based on these information, the FG Reporter generates a different report for each physical resource.

10.3 Workflow

In the previous sections we have described the essential components of the FG tool, here we present the workflow for the FG tool. The operation of the FG can be categorized into three main stages, which are:

1. Configuration: this is a design-time procedure for the QoS engineer to preconfigure the FG Analyzer through the MODAClouds IDE.
2. Analysis: this is a runtime step performed by the FG Analyzer with the Local DB.
3. Reporting/Updating: this is a step where the FG Reporter provides the developer with a report regarding the behavior of the application at runtime. The FG Actuator will also update the parameters of the QoS models given the output from FG Analyzer. This steps is performed after the application has already been running as it requires the results from the FG Analyzer.

The FG workflow is demonstrated in Fig. 10.2, which contains all the above three main stages. As mentioned in the previous section, the developer configures with the FG Analzyer through the MODAClouds IDE according to a configuration file, which is saved in the Object Store. The configuration file includes parameters such as the frequency to execute the FG Analyzer or the time period of the monitoring data to use. This configuration file is retrieved at deployment by the FG Analyzer. Then the Local DB periodically queries the Monitoring History DB to obtain the necessary information for the FG Analyzer. This data is passed to the FG Analzyer for the parameter estimation. With the estimation result, the FG Reporter will produce reports to the developer while the FG Actuator updates the QoS PCM models.

[2]http://www.dynamicreports.org/.

[3]https://community.jaspersoft.com/project/jasperreports-library.

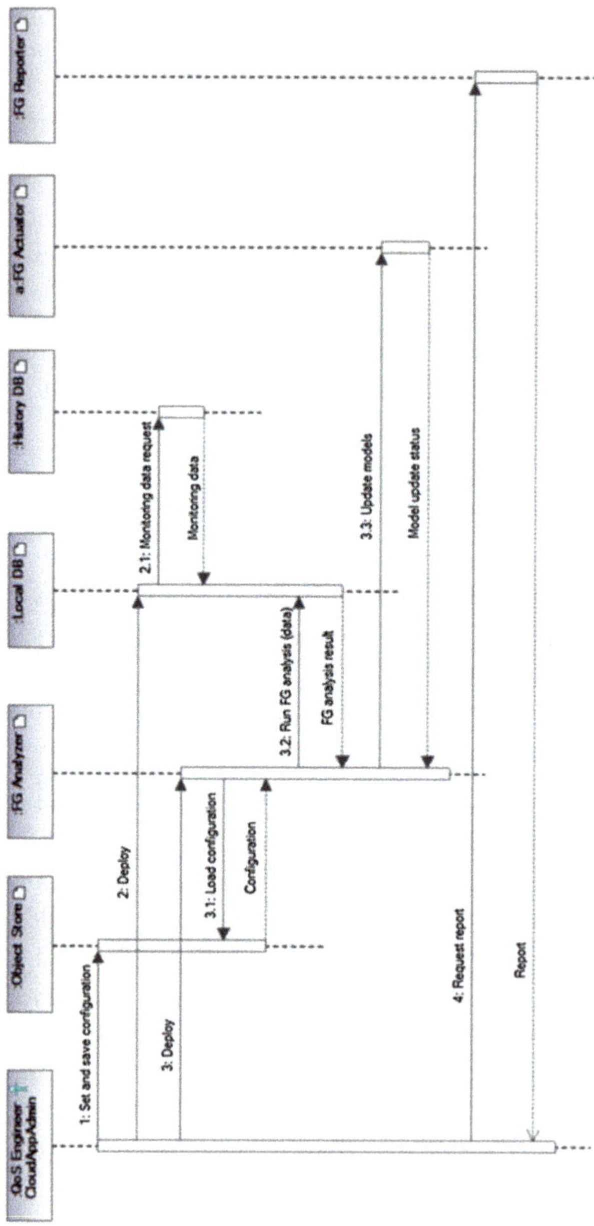

Fig. 10.2 Filling the gap workflow

10.4 Estimation Techniques for FG Analysis

10.4.1 A Bayesian Approach Based on Queue-Lengths

Closed queueing networks have been used for analyzing web applications [12, 17]. They are popular for example in software system modelling since complex applications are layered and the interactions between layers typically happen under admission control or finite threading limits.

The proposed GQL estimation method sets out to estimate the service demand placed by requests on the resources excluding contention due to other concurrently running requests. The service demand is normally difficult to obtain directly and requires inference. To provide these estimates, out method uses observations of the number of requests in each of the queueing stations, which makes it more applicable than utilization-based and response-based methods as the latter information may not be available in certain environments, such as PaaS deployments, or require deep instrumentation of the system.

Our method uses a Bayesian approach to estimate the mean demands, of which there has already been some attention in the recent literature [8, 18]. Still, with the exception of [18], classic Bayesian methods such as Markov-Chain Monte Carlo (MCMC) have not been applied before to the problem of queueing model parameter estimation. Even though the method in [18] is promising, it currently only applies to open queueing networks and single class systems. Our method, instead, is based on MCMC estimation with Gibbs sampling, and has the advantage of applying to closed multi-class models.

Figure 10.3 presents the experiment result for the GQL method with different number of classes of requests and queueing stations. The estimation error is computed as the mean relative difference between the estimated and the exact (known) value of the resource demand. From the figure, it can be noticed that the estimation error is under 10 %, showing the good accuracy of the GQL method. The execution time of

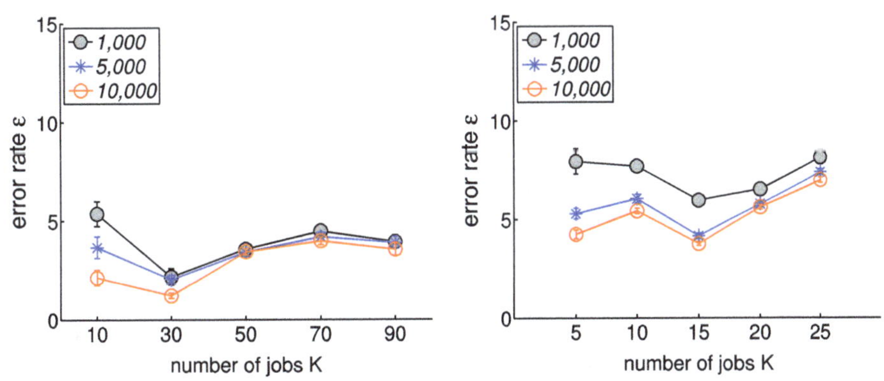

(a) 1 class, 1 station (b) 4 classes, 4 stations

Fig. 10.3 Mean estimation error for GQL

the GQL method depends on the input parameters of the developed algorithm. The running time for the presented case is 15 min, which shows that the algorithm is able to handle systems with a larger number of processing stations and request classes.

A detailed description of this method can be found in [19].

10.4.2 A Maximum-Likelihood Approach Based on Queue-Lengths and Response Times

Another proposed method, MINPS, is similar to the GQL presented in the previous section as MINPS also attempts to estimate the mean service demands placed by requests on the physical resources.

The performance model for MINPS is based on a multi-class queueing network with a single service station. It also considers the limit in the number of concurrent request in a station, which enables the analyzing of multi-threaded applications with limits on the number of threads in execution. A typical example is for applications running on a multi-threaded server, such as an application server or a servlet container with a preconfigured set of worker threads. Arriving requests to the application will stay in an admission buffer until a worker thread is available. We assume the admission control policy is first-come first-served and no workers are idle if there is a request staying in the admission buffer. Therefore the described performance model is indeed a closed queueing network similar as described in the previous section. Further, a request is able to change its class randomly after leaving the queueing station before entering the think time. This class-switching behavior represents systems where users may change the type of requests they generate.

The proposed MINPS estimation method is built on top of two new estimation approaches, RPS and MLPS. RPS is a regression based algorithm, which provides accurate estimation of mean service demand for multi-threaded application running on a single processor. For the multi-processor case, the proposed MLPS is able to solve this problem relying on a maximum likelihood demand estimation algorithm. MINPS integrates RPS and MLPS to produce accurate estimates at all loads of the multi-threaded applications.

MINPS differs from existing approaches in that, to the best of our knowledge, it is the first one to apply probabilistic descriptions in estimation problems for multi-threaded applications. For example, maximum likelihood estimations have been attempted only for simpler first-come first-served queues [8].

MINPS requires both queue lengths and response times as input metrics. These metrics can be obtained in several ways, e.g., the MODAClouds application-level data collectors, application server logs, internal application logs, etc.

Figure 10.4 demonstrates the mean estimation error of the MINPS method, compared with a baseline method CI with same sample size. As in the previous section, the estimation error is computed as the mean relative difference between the estimated and the exact (known) value of the resource demand. The CI method is an estimation method that requires the complete sample path of the requests, i.e. given

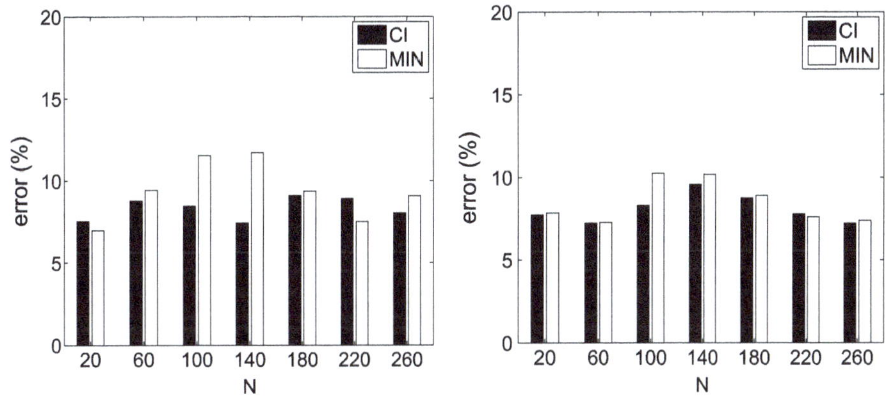

(a) 2 CPU, 8 worker threads (b) 4 CPU, 8 worker threads

Fig. 10.4 Mean estimation error for MINPS

a time window it knows all the points in time when a request is admitted and when it completes service. This information is difficult to collect, but it is useful to set a baseline for comparison, as both methods are assumed to make use of the same number of samples.

From Fig. 10.4, it can be noticed that the error of the MINPS and CI is similar, which reveals the accurate performance of MINPS. Although MINPS generates a larger estimation error, it is still under 15 %.

The execution time of MINPS depends on the model and obtained samples size and varies from 1 to 40 min for small models to large models. In light of this, the technique can be run periodically as part of the FG analysis.

A detailed description of these methods and additional validation results are provided in [16].

10.5 Conclusion

In this chapter we presented the MODAClouds Filling-the-Gap tool, which is a DevOps approach aiming to fulfill the gap development and operations. The FG tool supports a set of advanced algorithms for estimating the parameters of performance models at application runtime. Algorithms differ in the way that they take into consideration of different input monitoring metrics, which makes the tool useful particularly for application deployed in Cloud. It also features generating reports regarding the behavior of the application to give developers timely feedback of the system.

References

1. Roche J (2013) Adopting DevOps practices in quality assurance. Commun ACM 56:38–43

2. Rolia JA, Sevcik KC (1995) The method of layers. IEEE Trans Softw Eng 21(8):689–700
3. Kalbasi A, Krishnamurthy D, Rolia J, Dawson S (2012) Dec: service demand estimation with confidence. IEEE Trans Softw Eng 38:561–578
4. Kalbasi A, Krishnamurthy D, Rolia J, Richter M (2011) MODE: mix driven on-line resource demand estimation. In: Proceedings of IEEE CNSM
5. Wang W, Huang X, Qin X, Zhang W, Wei J, Zhong H (2012) Application-level CPU consumption estimation: towards performance isolation of multi-tenancy web applications. In: Proceedings of the 5th IEEE CLOUD
6. Cremonesi P, Dhyani K, Sansottera A (2010) Service time estimation with a refinement enhanced hybrid clustering algorithm. In: Analytical and stochastic modeling techniques and applications, ser. Lecture notes in computer science. Springer, Berlin
7. Cremonesi P, Sansottera A (2012) Indirect estimation of service demands in the presence of structural changes. In: QEST
8. Kraft S, Pacheco-Sanchez S, Casale G, Dawson S (2009) Estimating service resource consumption from response time measurements. In: Proceedings of the 4th VALUETOOLS
9. Kumar D, Zhang L, Tantawi A (2009) Enhanced inferencing: estimation of a workload dependent performance model. In: Proceeding of the 4th VALUETOOLS
10. Menascé D (2008) Computing missing service demand parameters for performance models. In: CMG 2008, pp 241–248
11. Pacifici G, Segmuller W, Spreitzer M, Tantawi A (2008) CPU demand for web serving: measurement analysis and dynamic estimation. Perform Eval 65:531–553
12. Zhang Q, Cherkasova L, Smirni E (2007) A regression-based analytic model for dynamic resource provisioning of multi-tier applications. In: Proceedings of the 4th ICAC. Washington, DC, USA. IEEE Computer Society, p 27ff
13. Zheng T, Woodside C, Litoiu M (2008) Performance model estimation and tracking using optimal filters. IEEE Trans Softw Eng 34:391–406
14. Ardagna D, Nitto ED, Casale G, Petcu D, Mohagheghi P, Mosser S, Matthews P, Gericke A, Ballagny C, D'Andria F (2012) Modaclouds: a model-driven approach for the design and execution of applications on multiple clouds. In: Proceedings of the 4th international workshop on modeling in software engineering
15. Liu Z, Wynter L, Xia CH, Zhang F (2006) Parameter inference of queueing models for IT systems using end-to-end measurements. Perform Eval 63(1):36–60
16. Pérez JF, Pacheco-Sanchez S, Casale G (2013) An offline demand estimation method for multi-threaded applications. In: MASCOTS, pp 21–30
17. Urgaonkar B, Pacifici G, Shenoy PJ, Spreitzer M, Tantawi AN (2005) An analytical model for multi-tier internet services and its applications. In: Proceedings of ACM SIGMETRICS. ACM Press, pp 291–302
18. Sutton C, Jordan MI (2011) Bayesian inference for queueing networks and modeling of internet services. Ann Appl Stat 5(1):254–282
19. Wang W, Casale G (2013) Bayesian service demand estimation using gibbs sampling. In: MASCOTS, pp 567–576

Chapter 11
Cloud Patterns

Teodor-Florin Fortiş and Nicolas Ferry

11.1 Introduction

A large number of design and architecture patterns have been identified during the last years, as the Cloud technologies were finding their path to maturity. In [1] Fehling et al., the authors expose a basic pattern-oriented view on Cloud computing, together with relevant patterns, view which is also applicable in the case of multi-Cloud applications.

Another set of more than forty patterns are included in the AWS Cloud Design patterns (CDP) [2], offering "*a collection of solutions and design ideas for using AWS Cloud technology to solve common systems design problems*".

In addition to the core set of Cloud design patterns, Erl et al. [3] propose a set of compound patterns, which, for most of them, are related to the essential characteristics of Cloud computing, such as Cloud bursting, elastic environment, multi-tenancy, Cloud deployment models, and others.

The IBM RedPaper [4] offers some insights on Pure Application Systems patterns and virtual application patterns (VAPs) which are "*a new Cloud deployment model that represents an evolution of the traditional topology patterns that are supported in virtual system patterns*". Finally, the Microsoft point of view on development of Cloud-hosted applications is covered by Homer et al. [5].

Complementary to the numerous design and architecture patterns that have already been described in the literature, a set of design heuristics or success factors was fully

T.-F. Fortiş (✉)
Institute e-Austria Timişoara and West University of Timişoara,
B-dul Vasile Pârvan 4, 300223 Timişoara, Romania
e-mail: fortis@info.uvt.ro

N. Ferry
Stiftelsen SINTEF, Postboks 4760, Sluppen, 7465 Trondheim, Norway
e-mail: nicolas.ferry@sintef.no

E. Di Nitto et al. (eds.), *Model-Driven Development and Operation of Multi-Cloud Applications*, PoliMI SpringerBriefs,
DOI 10.1007/978-3-319-46031-4_11

described in the context of the MODAClouds approach. This set will help mitigate various pitfalls when designing multi-Cloud applications.

11.2 Motivational Guidance

Important design heuristics and guidances have been identified as highly relevant for multi-Cloud applications, and especially in the context of MODAClouds.

Compute Partitioning

Compute partitioning is a design heuristic that helps building systems that can easily be maintained and deployed on Cloud platforms and infrastructures and advocates the utilization of patterns such as *loose coupling*, *compute partitioning*, *distributed applications* or *integration provider*. It allows application developers to efficiently exploit resources that can be provisioned with minimal effort. Particularly, as Cloud applications usually rely on multiple distributed resources, modularity and loose coupling become central for efficient exploitation of Cloud properties.

Thus, the separation of concern principle is essential in order to achieve the distribution of resources, as multi-Cloud application usually rely on resources possibly offered by multiple providers with their own specificities. This principle advocates decomposing and encapsulating the features of an application into modular and reusable blocks.

Based on the *computing partitioning guidance* [5] and using the *loose coupling* and *distribution application* patterns [1], the MODACloudML proposal is to decompose applications into logical components and help the user in allocating and reusing these components on Cloud resources.

Multiple Datacentre Deployment

Multiple datacentre deployment is one of the key factors that ensures successful deployments across multiple Cloud providers. This design heuristic relies on the *loose coupling* and *multiple datacentre deployment* patterns.

In the case of multi-Cloud applications, the providers of these applications will attempt to identify and exploit particularities of the underlying Cloud solutions in order to achieve an optimization of various characteristics (e.g., performance, availability, cost, etc.). Developers of such applications may therefore need novel design approaches in order to fully benefit from the varying sets of services that are supported by the different Cloud providers.

The approach considered in the case of MODAClouds consists in a separation of the design of the application from the technical specification of the underlying infrastructure as suggested by the MDA architecture. To achieve this separation, Cloud provider-independent models (CPIM) and Cloud provider-specific models (CPSM) are considered. The first ones enable the specification of Cloud provider-independent deployment scenarios in a Cloud agnostic way whilst the second allows selecting Cloud provider specific resources. CPIM should provide an appropriate level of abstraction to allow the generation of CPSM, targeting various providers and being aware of their specificity at the same time. The identification of the right level of abstraction, as well as of the concepts that are relevant at the level of each of these models generates specific challenges in this scenario.

Instrumentation and Telemetry

Instrumentation and telemetry are key success factors in building feedback about the runtime performance of the system and its underlying platform and infrastructure. *Instrumentation and telemetry*, *loose coupling*, and *multiple datacentre deployment* are the most important patterns involved.

While in the case of a simple Cloud-application collecting some metrics related to the Cloud resources through provider's platform APIs may provide the right perspective on the behaviour of the application, this is not necessarily the case for multi-Cloud applications. Monitoring interfaces are likely to be incompatible and provider-specific, and therefore the monitoring activities could be subject to vendor lock-in. Moreover, it might not be enough to only monitor Cloud resource's usage in order to measure application's resource consumption and to provide efficient resource management activities.

Consequently, the MODAClouds approach supports this guidance and offer the means, at the level of the design-time platform and of the monitoring platform, to (i) allow the definition of monitoring rules at both the infrastructure and application levels in a provider-independent way, and (ii) enable the design of monitoring rules describing how incoming stream of data have to be processed, and what output should be produced when certain conditions have been verified.

11.3 MODAClouds-Specific Patterns

The guidance and design heuristics that were briefly described in Sect. 11.2 relate to an important number of Cloud design and architecture patterns, of which some can be adopted without major changes in a multi-Cloud context. However, a subset was specifically extended and adapted in the MODAClouds context to better support the design of multi-Cloud applications. We briefly describe these patterns in the following subsections.

External Configuration Store

The *external configuration store* pattern propose to outsource configuration and deployment information for any component or services of the system into separate services thus improving reusability and flexibility in the deployment and/or configuration process of application components. This pattern, as depicted in Fig. 11.1, extends the *configuration store pattern* [5] and it partially involves other patterns and mechanisms, like the *resource management system* mechanism [3].

In the case of MODAClouds, the configuration of a multi-Cloud application does not only include properties associated to the functional behavior of the application,

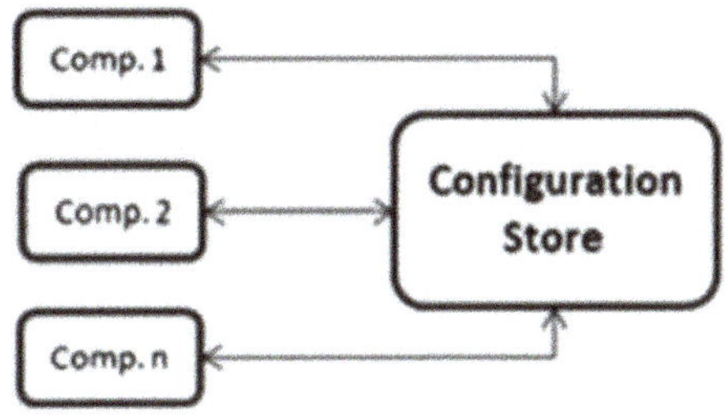

Fig. 11.1 The external configuration store pattern

but also provisioning and deployment information for the underlying infrastructure. Accordingly, the configuration store pattern was extended to include the overall information required for the deployment and configuration process of the multi-Cloud application. Therefore, one can achieve an externalization of the configuration and deployment information for any particular components or services into a separate service.

The use of this pattern could be relevant in various situations, like: (i) when the application contains several instances of the same component (or group of components), whose configuration must be synchronized; (ii) the configuration of the various components will have to be dynamically adjusted to accommodate various load and/or usage patterns; (iii) when similar reconfigurations need to be triggered on several parts of the application.

Leader-Followers

The aim of the *leaders-followers* pattern (or leader election pattern, see also [5]) is to dynamically delegate the management of subparts of the architecture to a separate component that has been elected. Such a feature is particularly relevant when Cloud applications aggregate several subsystems, with an appropriate level of complexity, such that the total complexity exceeds the capacity of a single management entity.

In a multi-Cloud context, the leader-followers pattern enables the election for each Cloud of a single component responsible for configuring and managing subparts of the execution environment. Thus, the leader (a master node) will have the necessary knowledge of its peers, managing their configurations accordingly.

This pattern is relevant especially (i) when the application contains numerous instances of the same component (or group of components), whose configuration and deployment must be synchronized, as in Fig. 11.2; (ii) when massive and simultaneous updates are necessary for instances of the same group of components.

Runtime Reconfiguration

The intent behind the *runtime reconfiguration* pattern is to dynamically reconfigure application components and frameworks as well as their execution environments to minimize the downtime in a production setting. This pattern is extended from the pattern with the same name from [5] to the dynamic adaptation of the application deployment using the `models@runtime` architecture. The use of this pattern together with the `models@runtime` architecture enables third-parties to adapt only selected parts of the deployment whilst minimizing the downtime for the rest of the application.

Specific interest exists around this pattern especially when an application or the deployment of an application needs to be reconfigured dynamically at runtime, such as adapting logging policies, updating database connections, deploying new services, and others.

Particularly, in the case of MODAClouds, the `models@runtime` engine maintains a MODACloudML deployment model causally connected to the running system, and: (i) any modification to the CPIM will be reflected in the CPSM and propagated on-demand onto the running system; (ii) any change in the running system will be reflected in the CPSM, which, in turn, can be assessed with respect to the CPIM. Furthermore, by using the aforementioned deployment model, the `models@runtime` environment enables reducing the gap between the runtime and design-time activities.

Provider Adapter

In the case of multi-Cloud application it is highly important that the implementation of various components remain unmodified to the specificities of different Cloud environments. The *provider adapter* pattern offers the means for a smooth transition of applications and components from one Cloud provider to another.

The *provider adapter* pattern is highly relevant in the context of multi-Cloud applications, and it has been applied to the MODACloudML supporting tools and extended to the language itself through the concept of Cloud provider-independent

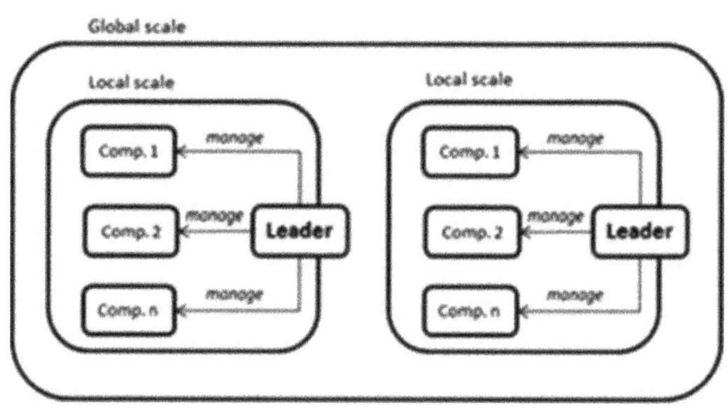

Fig. 11.2 The leader-followers pattern

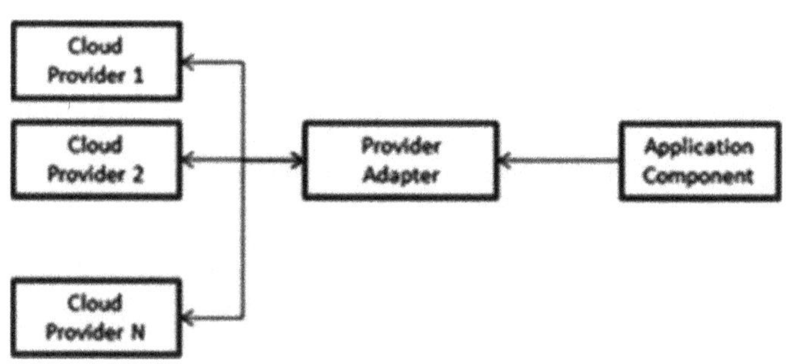

Fig. 11.3 The provider-adapter pattern

models that can be automatically or semi-automatically refined into Cloud provider-specific models.

This pattern is especially relevant when application components are not written for a specific single Cloud provider, and may move to or across other providers for maintenance reasons for instance (see also Fig. 11.3).

11.4 Conclusions

In this chapter we provided an overview of the set of guidances and patterns that have been defined or extended during the MODAClouds project on the basis of the experience gained in designing and managing multi-Cloud applications. All of them have been successfully applied during the project to support the design of both the MODAClouds tools and case studies. These patterns complement well the large set of existing pattern already available in the literature.

References

1. Fehling C, Leymann F, Retter R, Schupeck W, Arbitter P (2014) Cloud computing patterns—fundamentals to design, build, and manage cloud applications. Springer
2. AWS cloud design patterns. http://en.clouddesignpattern.org/index.php
3. Erl T, Cope R, Naserpour A (2015) Cloud computing design patterns. Prentice Hall/Pearson PTR. http://cloudpatterns.org/
4. Brandle C, Grose V, Hong MY, Imholz J, Kaggali P, Mantegazza M (2014) Cloud computing patterns of expertise. IBM RedPaper. http://www.redbooks.ibm.com/redpapers/pdfs/redp5040.pdf
5. Homer A, Sharp J, Brader L, Narumoto M, Swanson T (2014) Cloud design patterns: prescriptive architecture guidance for cloud applications (Microsoft patterns & practices). MSDN Library. https://msdn.microsoft.com/en-us/library/dn568099.aspx

Chapter 12
Modelio Project Management Server Constellation

Antonin Abhervé and Marcos Almeida

12.1 Introduction

SOFTEAM is a French middle-sized company that provides the Modelio modelling tool. Modelio.[1] is an enterprise-level open source modelling solution delivering functionality for business, software and infrastructure architects. It is a comprehensive MDE workbench tool supporting the UML2.x standard. Modelio provides a csentral IDE which allows various languages (represented as UML profiles) to be combined in the same model. Modelio proposes various extension modules, enabling the customization of this MDE environment for different purposes and stakeholders.

The **Team Work Manager** is SOFTEAM's solution to team collaboration in Modelio. It allows Modelio users, after a minimal software and hardware investment, to efficiently share and work together on models stored in a central repository accessible in a local network or in the Internet. It automates version control and configuration management, making sure every developer has access to the last version of the shared model and works on a uniform configuration. From the point of view of the developer, a repository is divided into Projects, which contain: Model elements, Extension modules used by the user and Configuration information. A repository needs to be installed, configured and maintained by the users in private machines. A SVN repository may store different projects and different teams may work in the same repository. Developers use the Modelio desktop client to access a central repository on a SVN like workflow: committing modifications to model elements,

[1] http://www.modelio.org.

A. Abhervé (✉) · M. Almeida
Softeam Cadextan, 21 Avenue Victor Hugo, 75016 Paris, France
e-mail: antonin.abherve@softeam.fr

M. Almeida
e-mail: marcos.almeida@softeam.fr

E. Di Nitto et al. (eds.), *Model-Driven Development and Operation of Multi-Cloud Applications*, PoliMI SpringerBriefs,
DOI 10.1007/978-3-319-46031-4_12

receiving updates from other users and using merges/locks to deal with concurrent work.

By its participation on the MODAClouds project, SOFTEAM intended to move its modelling services to the Cloud in order to relieve the burden for our clients in supporting the necessary infrastructure. During the MODAClouds project, we developed a new version of this tool called **Constellation** [1, 2]. This service is based on a Service-Oriented Architecture under which the TeamWork Manager is provided as a service on the Cloud. By the beginning of the third year of the project we started providing commercial services based on Constellation.

We hope that the "potentially infinite" resources available on the Cloud will make tasks such as scaling the servers of a project up and out and moving between different Cloud providers very easy to our customers. Additionally, activities such as monitoring and adapting the installation hopefully will be able to be executed without specialized knowledge in systems administration.

The MODAClouds provided features have an important role in fulfilling these objectives. As we are going to present in the following sections, the role of MODAClouds in Constellation is two-fold. At design time, MODAClouds should support design and implementation in a Cloud provider independent way, reducing development costs, and increasing its flexibility. At run time, it should support the monitoring and adaptation of the application to support its desired QoS levels.

This chapter is organised as follows. Section 12.2 presents the proposed architecture of Constellation. Section 12.3 presents how we used MODAClouds components in building our case study. Finally, Sect. 12.4 presents our conclusions.

12.2 Proposed Architecture

In order to simplify this migration, the architecture of our Cloud solution relies on the implementation of a component called **Administration Server** (Fig. 12.1). The Administration Server allows clients to create and manage user accounts, define roles, and create modelling projects and associate users and roles to specific projects. The Administration Server is designed as a JEE application which provides a web accessible user interface support implemented with Java Server Faces 2 and service behaviour supported by Entity Java Beans components. This application is linked with an relational database to ensure persistency of application data.

The Administration Server can provision computing resources in order to maintain the established level of quality of service. Cloud Services managed by a Administration Server are delivered as Cloud-enabled applications. These applications are deployed on the provisioned Cloud resource. Once deployed in Cloud resources, services usually need to be configured and accessed by clients. The Administration Server needs to make sure that the necessary projects, users and permissions have been created and set up once a Cloud agent has been installed. Standard protocols are used for both activities. Web Services enable the deployed agents to be configured. Moreover, TCP/IP protocols will allow Modelio desktop based clients to connect to an agent, independently from which Cloud it has been deployed.

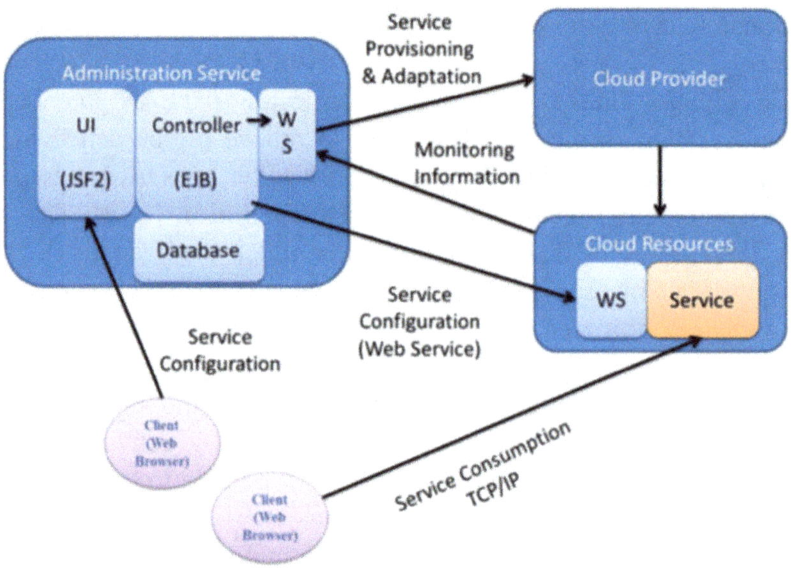

Fig. 12.1 The architecture of the administration server

External agents are independent applications that provide specific high resource consuming services to Prototype of Constellation. Agents can be deployed on demand on specific Cloud instances (IaaS or PaaS depending on their implementation). The number of deployed agents may change in real time depending on the application workload. Each agent implements a variable number of services called **Workers**, which are executed when an agent receives a command from the Administration server.

The only dependency of this design to the specific Cloud provider is the communication between the Administration Server and the Cloud provider in order to deploy, monitor and eventually migrate services. The actual code to interact with the Cloud provider is however encapsulated in a Web Service usually installed on the Administration Server. This Web Service translates actual requests from the user into specific requests to MODAClouds runtime components.

12.3 Use of MODAClouds Design and Runtime Components

12.3.1 Modelling with Creator 4Clouds

We used MODAClouds Creator 4Clouds Functional Modelling tool to describe the architecture of Constellarion's Administration Server along with its modelling services. We have also used this model as input to other design and runtime tools. During the first MODAClouds phase we considered two kinds of services: **SVN** and **HTTP**

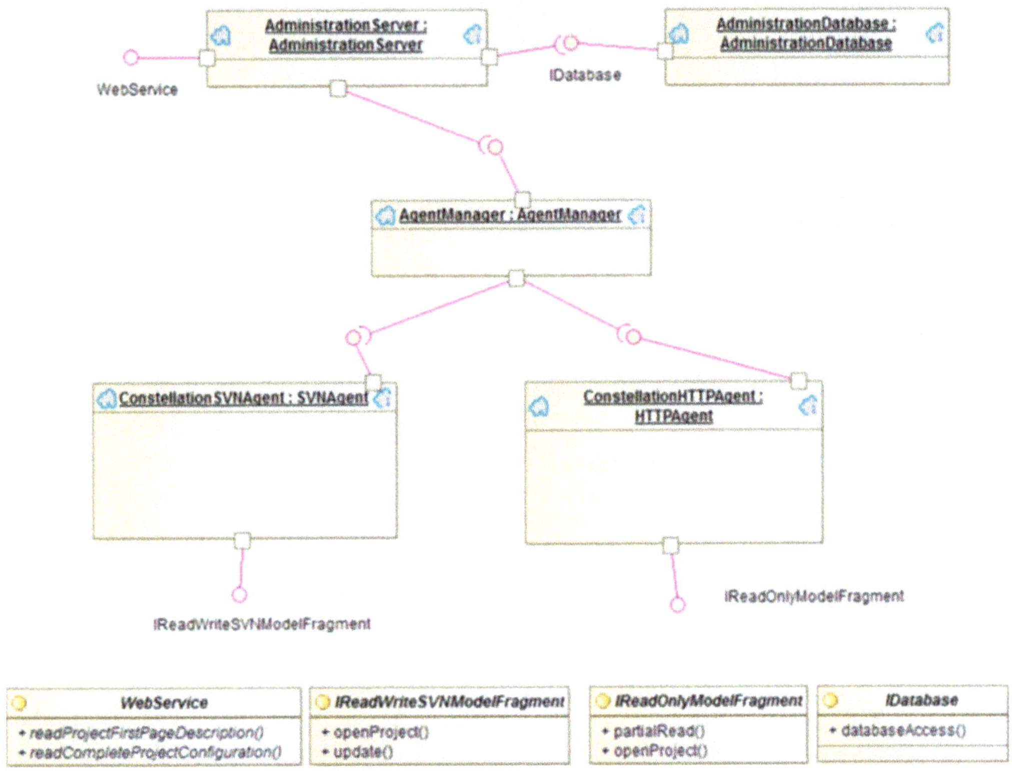

Fig. 12.2 Case study CCIM modelling on the IDE

fragments. The first one provides a read-write model that is edited collaboratively, while the second one provides read-only models that are shared among different teams.

Figure 12.2 depicts the functional architecture of Constellation specified with the MODAClouds IDE as a Cloud Computation Independent Model.

At the highest level, the CCIM shows the services that compose Constellation: the Administration Server and the Administration Database connected by an interface provided by the Administration Database and required by the Administration Server.

Still at the CCIM level, Fig. 12.3 shows the QoS constraints associated with the most important operations provided by the Constellation modelling services. For

	metric	unit	aggregationType	rangeMin	rangeMax
HTTPAgentReadModelAverage	ResponseTime	ms	Average		5000
HTTPAgentReadModelPercentile	ResponseTime	ms	Percentile(thPercentile=85)		12000

	metric	unit	aggregationType	rangeMin	rangeMax
SVNAgentReadModelAverage	ResponseTime	ms	Average		15000
SVNAgentReadModelPercentile	ResponseTime	ms	Percentile(thPercentile=85)		30000
SVNAgentWriteModelAverage	ResponseTime	ms	Average		60000
SVNAgentWriteModelPercentile	ResponseTime	ms	Percentile(thPercentile=85)		300000

Fig. 12.3 CCIM QoS constraints on MODAClouds IDE

SVN fragments, 15 s is the target average time for reading model modifications, and 60 s is the target average time for writes. This considers that users make large commits (i.e., containing a great number of model changes, and therefore expect to obtain large change sets when they update). For HTTP models, 5 s is the average time for reading parts of the model, considering that users make infrequent accesses to subparts of shared read-only models. Constraints on the 85th percentile are used to define acceptable upper bounds for response times. These are set to 12 s for HTTP reads, and to 30 s and 5 min for SVN reads and writes, respectively.

CPIM and CPSM models describe the deployment of the application at different levels of abstraction, first in a Cloud provider independent way, and then in a Cloud provider specific way. Figure 12.4 presents excerpts of the Constellation application model described in MODACloudML at the three levels of abstraction in order to illustrate the correspondence between the CCIM and the CPIM and CPSM models.

12.3.2 Multi-cloud Deployment with CloudML 4Clouds

The deployment model at CPIM level allows us to model the deployment of our application by identifying the various components of our application deployment.

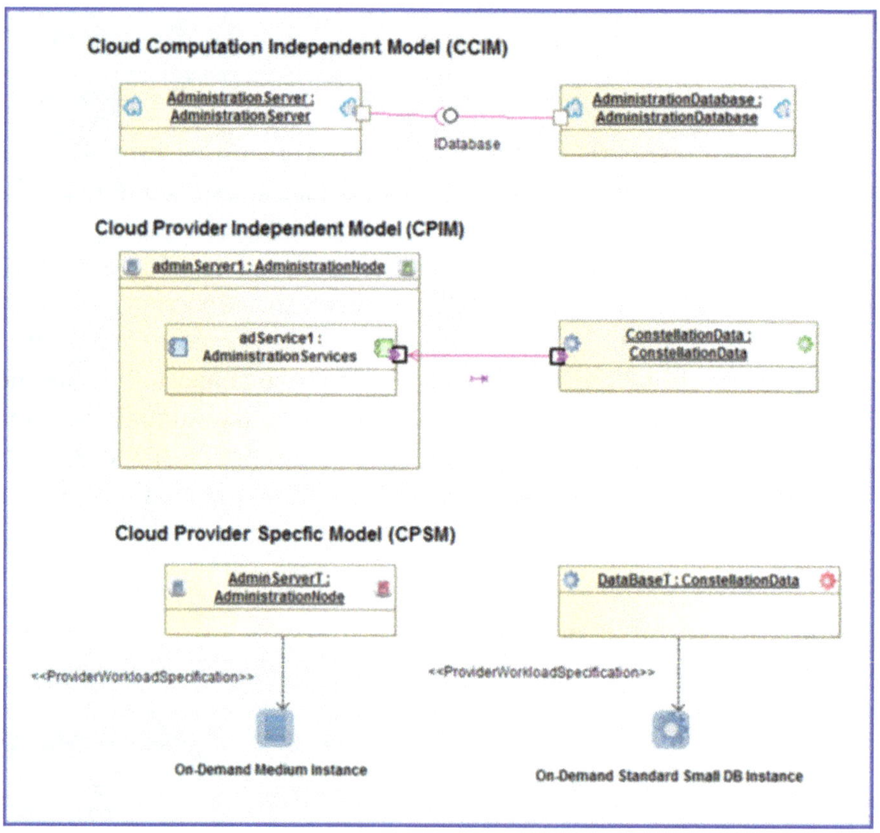

Fig. 12.4 Three levels in IDE

In this experiment, our efforts focused on better use of Cloud platforms through the integration of PaaS services and the migration to a multi-Cloud deployment solution. In a second step, we sought to take advantage of the support of multi-Cloud environments allowed by the MODAClouds project. We studied the best deployment configuration for our application and selected three Cloud providers: Amazon EC2, Flexiant and Amazon RDS.

Figure 12.5 describes the deployment of Constellation in a multi-Cloud context. It shows an Administration Server and two agents, both of them in IaaS Cloud nodes. The former in Amazon, the later in Flexiant. The database that stores administration data is stored on a PaaS database, provided by Amazon RDS.

This development brings the following benefits:

- Allows us to scale the compute and storage resources available to our database to meet Constellation needs.
- Provides the best reliability to our application with automated backups, DB snapshots and automatic host replacement capabilities.
- Provides predictable and consistent performance for I/O intensive transactional database workloads.

12.3.3 *Cost and Performance Analysis with SPACE 4Clouds*

As part of MODACloudsML CCIM models, we provided models of how users interact with Constellation, and of the performance of Constellation services when actually deployed on a virtual machines. We used SPACE4 Clouds to assess the costs and

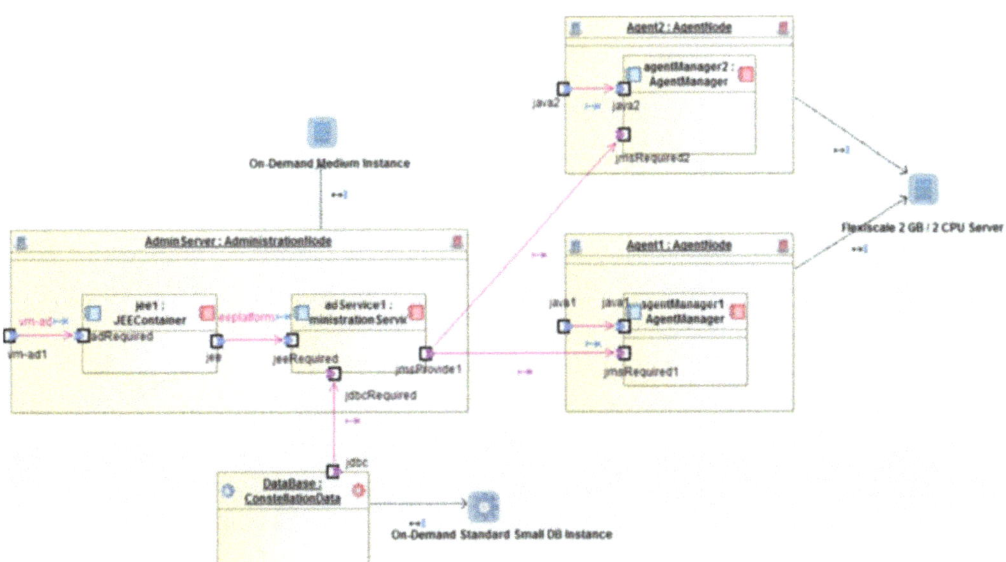

Fig. 12.5 Constellation deployment in multi-cloud environments

QoS the current architecture is able to provide on different Clouds, and in particular, the maximum number of clients we can serve with the modelled architecture.

In addition, we devised a trial architecture for a new modelling service called **Conference Service** to be implemented during the last year of the project, and compared its QoS characteristics with the one implemented in the first two years of the project. Differently from a SVN service, the conference service decouples the reading and writing load on the system in different VMs that can be load balanced and Cloud bursted independently. This is a typical example of advanced deployment configurations Constellation needs to support. Our experiments showed that the Conference Service is more scalable than the current solution.

The Fig. 12.6 presents the usage model of our users, obtained through observation of typical users. It considers users that connect to modelling through their full workday. Five percent of the time they interact with Constellation, they connect to an existing project, which is translated onto the sequence of calls we see on the top of the figure. Ten percent of the time, they read updates from an SVN model, seventy-five percent of the time they get data from HTTP fragments and ten percent of the time they perform SVN commits.

In addition to usage models, we provided models of user workload throughout the day (see the Fig. 12.7). We represented a typical business office workload, with most of it concentrated around commercial working hours (8–12 h and 13–17 h).

SPACE 4Clouds allowed us to discover the peak number of users supported by this architecture. Figure 12.8 shows the result of this analysis. We can see that the SVN service supports around 250–300 users without breaking QoS constraints, while the Conference service scales to almost the double number of users without breaking constraints.

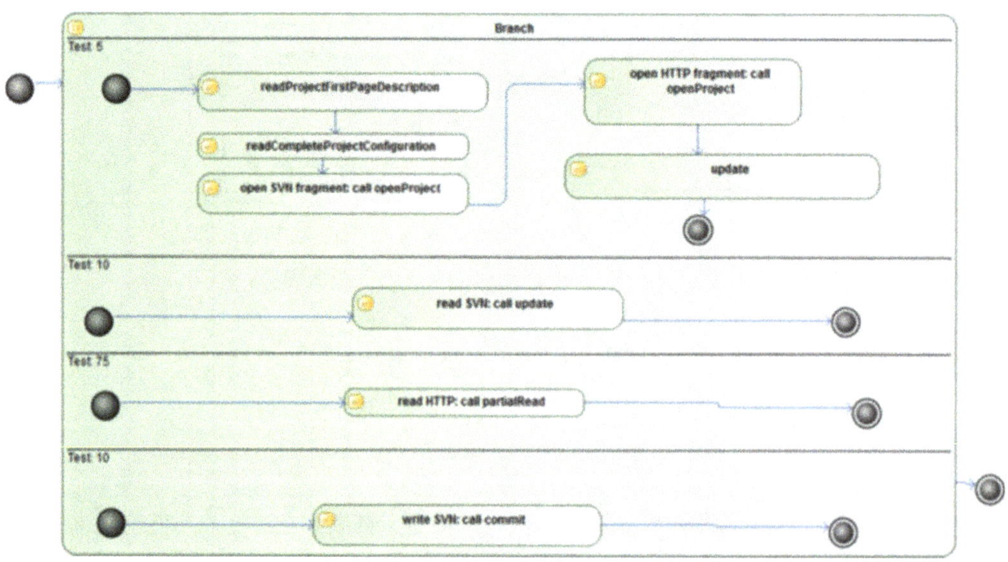

Fig. 12.6 Modelling constellation user's behavior

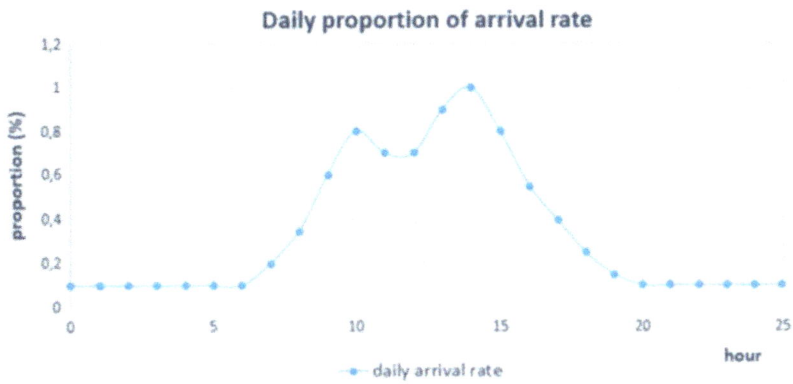

Fig. 12.7 Modelling constellation user's workload

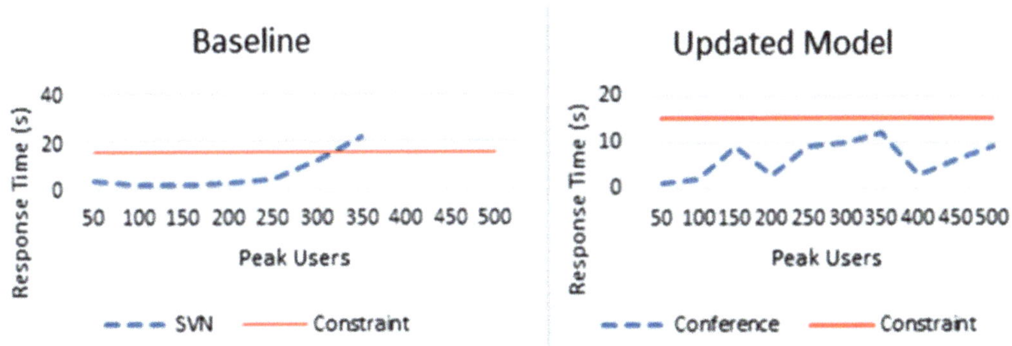

Fig. 12.8 Response time bottleneck estimations for SVN and conference services

12.3.4 *Multi-cloud Monitoring and Management with Energizer 4Clouds*

Energizer 4Clouds provides valuable services for our case study, such as the management of the execution, intended as the set of operations to instantiate; run and stop services on the Cloud; the monitoring of the running application and the self-adaptation of the application, to ensure the fulfilment of the QoS goals.

When defining the final design of the Constellation case study, we were interested in the best way to integrate the features provided by the platform into our application. In the context of the Constellation case study, we are interested in the integration of three aspects of Energizer 4Clouds: the monitoring platform, the self-adaptation platform and the execution platform. Figure 12.9 presents the deployment model of the Constellation case study including runtime platform components.

The Monitoring Platform allows us to monitor specific metrics collected from business components of our case study deployed on different Cloud platforms. To achieve this goal, we integrated five components into our architecture: three componentsfrom the monitoring platform and two components developed using the API

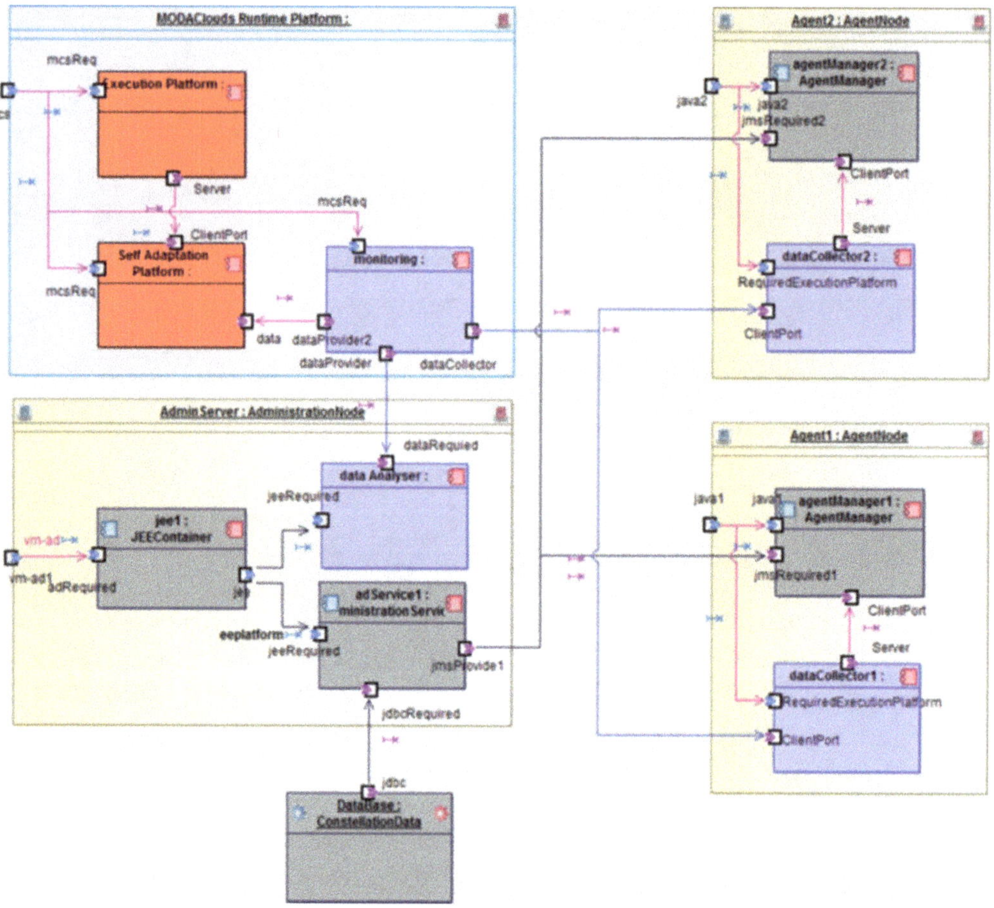

Fig. 12.9 MODAClouds runtime platform integration

provided by platform components. The role of these is to exploit monitoring data in our application.

To exploit the monitoring platform, we have integrated two components based on the API provided by the monitoring platform. These components ensure the intermediation between the monitoring platforms and business components of Constellation. They allowed us to implement a Cloud vendor independent agent monitoring user interface, and to integrate it to our commercial offering.

- **Constellation Data Collector**: To collect business metrics from Constellation agents, we integrated into our architecture this extension of the monitoring platform. Based on MODAClouds Data Collector API, this programme will collect data about CPU, RAMS and Access Disk of each process managed by agents.
- **Constellation Data Analyzer**: Based on the REST API of MODAClouds Monitoring Manage, Constellation will incorporate a component to analyse, store and display monitoring data according to a business point of view. This service will be integrated into the Administration Server.

12.4 Conclusion

Constellation can be presented as an advanced repository which stores the models defined using the Modelio CASE tool and which provides several high-time consuming services on the Cloud. Among its services, we find the creation of collaborative projects, the hosting of model fragments allowing teamwork, the management of a Model Library catalogue or monitoring services applied to all these elements.

In this chapter, we presented the final version of the Project Management Server, renamed, for commercial reasons to Constellation. The development of Constellation started with the beginning of the MODAClouds project and by the end of it we have a first version that started to be commercialized. The current commercial version of Constellation is restricted to deployment on customer premises. We are confident that, thanks to MODAClouds, its architecture is ready to the Cloud.

The Constellation case study integrated both design time and runtime components from MODAClouds in its design. At design time, MODAClouds supported the design of the architecture of the application, and its early QoS analysis, in order to identify bottlenecks. At runtime, MODAClouds supported the multi-Cloud deployment, management and monitoring of Constellation.

References

1. Almeida Da Silva MA, Abhervé A, Sadovykh A (2013) From the desktop to the multiclouds: the case of ModelioSaaS. In: 15th international symposium on symbolic and numeric algorithms for scientific computing (SYNASC), 23–26 Sep 2013, pp 462–472
2. Desfray P (2015) Model repositories at the enterprises and systems scale the Modelio constellation solution. In: 2015 3rd international conference on model-driven engineering and software development (MODELSWARD), Feb 2015, pp IS–15

Chapter 13
BPM in the Cloud: The BOC Case

Alexander Gunka, Harald Kuehn and Stepan Seycek

13.1 Introduction

To move an existing application to a Cloud-based operating model is a challenging task. This chapter presents a real life case in this domain. It is based on a case study from BOC which uses MODAClouds technology to enact four major use cases for the Cloud deployment of the BPM tool ADONIS. The first use case describes the provider selection in a multi-Cloud environment based on the decision support system Venues 4Clouds. In the second use case CloudML4Clouds is used to implement a model-based Cloud deployment procedure. The third use case shows the usage of Tower 4Clouds for real-time monitoring spanning various system levels to enable DevOps engineers to gather their custom monitoring metrics. The fourth use case describes the Cloud-to-Cloud migration process including the implemented approach for data migration aspects.

13.2 Context and Motivation

BOC group is a medium-sized software and consultancy company providing products and services for Business Process Management (BPM), Enterprise Architecture Management (EAM) and Governance, Risk, Compliance (GRC). BOC originated

A. Gunka · H. Kuehn · S. Seycek (✉)
BOC Information Technologies Consulting GmbH, Operngasse 20b,
1040 Vienna, Austria
e-mail: stepan.seycek@boc-group.com

A. Gunka
e-mail: alexander.gunka@boc-group.com

H. Kuehn
e-mail: harald.kuehn@boc-group.com

E. Di Nitto et al. (eds.), *Model-Driven Development and Operation of Multi-Cloud Applications*, PoliMI SpringerBriefs,
DOI 10.1007/978-3-319-46031-4_13

1995 as a spin-off company from the University of Vienna, Department Knowledge Engineering. Since then, BOC has grown to one of the leading companies within these domains, established operations in various European countries and maintains a world-wide customer base. In all their activities, BOC follows a model-driven approach.

ADOxx is BOC's meta-modelling platform for implementing the modelling products of the BOC Management Office by defining domain specific meta-models, by configuring specific behavior and adding functionality to complement a given methodology. Business users of the products can manage their model and object repositories in a collaborative way leveraging highly adaptable versioning and release workflows. They can create analytical views, define custom queries, and generate various reports interacting via web-based graphical editors and dashboards.

While most enterprise software is still deployed on-premises, Software-as-a-Service is expected to grow rapidly over the next years. According to IDC the total Cloud software market will grow to surpass $100 billion by 2018 at a compound annual growth rate of 21.3 %. In order to be able to benefit from these new opportunities and from the advantages in terms of resilience, agility and cost efficiency the Cloud promises, BOC committed to a strategy for providing their applications as SaaS in addition to their existing sales and operation models. In order to minimize risks BOC decided to apply an iterative process to achieve this target [1]). Technology developed within the MODAClouds project plays an important role in achieving this step of business model extension.

As one of the first steps implementing this strategy, a prototypical instantiation of a process modelling language using the ADOxx meta-modelling platform has been ported to the Cloud with the help of tools and methodologies developed within MODAClouds. Based on the results of this evaluation, BOC has recently moved the solution to production environment by launching ADONIS:cloud [2].

13.3 Application Scenario

During the process of defining requirements to be supported by MODAClouds, four main use cases (depicted in Fig. 13.1) were identified with regard to BOC's application scenario. First, the *selection of Cloud providers* should be simplified with the help of decision support tools and methodologies. After this step MODAClouds should provide assistance to *deploy* a given application stack to selected Clouds in an automated, Cloud provider independent way. Advanced *monitoring* techniques should then be used to track system health and quality of service. In case of detected violations another *cloud provider* would be *selected* and the application should be *re-deployed* to the new provider. In addition, data would be *migrated* and traffic would be switched to the new deployment.

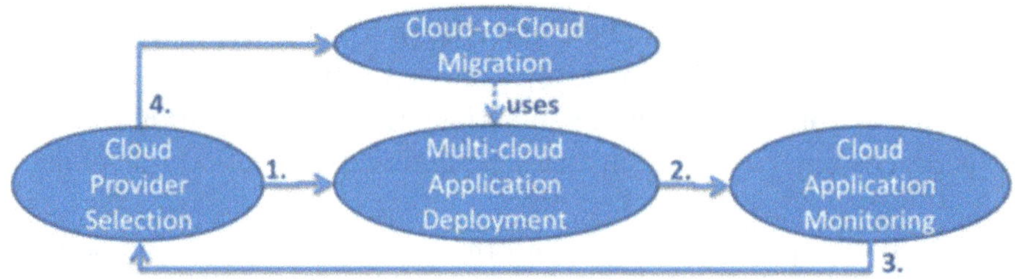

Fig. 13.1 BOC's main use cases to be supported by MODAClouds to offer ADONIS as SaaS

13.3.1 Cloud Provider Selection

Soon after the decision to offer the BPM solution ADONIS as SaaS, BOC was facing the challenge of selecting an appropriate IaaS provider. They started the decision making process by collecting various decision criteria taking into account operations, legal, cost, and sales related aspects. They assigned relative weights to these criteria and marked some of them as must-have features. As a next step around 20 candidate providers were considered and rated first only considering the must-have criteria which helped reducing efforts in data collection by ruling out a large portion of the initial candidates list. For the remaining candidates the rest of the data was collected and the three providers with the highest rankings were presented to the decision team for discussion.

Retrospectively some of the weaknesses of this intuitive approach soon became obvious [3]:

- The cost of re-evaluating the providers on a regular basis in order to improve quality of service and cost efficiency would be very high.
- The goal of covering different markets will require addressing strict data location policies and therefore the ability to deploy to multiple Clouds. These aspects are hard to address using the initial approach since it would require a much larger number of providers to be analysed resulting in very high efforts in data gathering and analysis.
- The criteria chosen intuitively based on BOC's own experience were not comprehensive enough to cover all relevant aspects.
- In particular, the ease of migration from one provider to another, which should have been considered as one of the most important criteria, was ignored.

BOC contributed these experiences during the requirements elicitation process for Venues 4Clouds, MODAClouds Decision Making System for Cloud Service Offer Selection which is described in detail in Chap. 2 [add reference]. In particular, BOC contributed a number of functional requirements, an initial set of decision criteria, and general success criteria for a Decision Support System to be developed [4].

Based on the requirements gathered, a risk-driven framework for decision support [3], a methodology for eliciting risk, cost and quality aspects in multi-Cloud environments [5, 6], and a prototype of a Decision Support System (DSS) have

Table 13.1 Stakeholders and assets considered in the DSS

Stakeholders	Type of intangible asset	Assets considered
Business representatives	Business oriented intangible assets	Customer loyalty, legislation compliance, internal efficiency and performance, sales rate, market awareness, improve product innovation and quality
Technical (DevOps) representatives	Technology oriented intangible assets	Data privacy, data integrity, maintainability, end user performance, service availability, cost stability

been developed. BOC used this methodology and the prototypical DSS to perform a light weight risk analysis by first defining a set of relevant business-oriented and technology oriented assets, determining risks related to these assets, and treatments mitigating these risks [4]). During this assessment process both business and technical stakeholders were involved. Table 13.1 lists the assets considered by either of these stakeholders.

In that way, for example customer *loyalty*, which was identified as an important asset by business representatives, has been related to the technical oriented assets *data privacy*, *data integrity*, *end user performance*, and *service availability*. *Data privacy*, in turn, has been related to the risks *unauthorized access from IaaS provider*, *insufficient isolation*, *insufficient physical security*, and *data exposure to government authorities*. As possible mitigations for these risks the *availability of certificates guaranteeing information security* and the *possibility to select a specific data location* were selected. A complete mapping of all identified assets, risks and mitigations can be found in the appendix of MODAClouds public deliverable 2.3.2 [7].

The fact that the user is guided through a structured process, starting with high level assets helped to identify a larger set of risks and, consequently, treatments to be considered, that would not have been detected using the original intuitive approach. At the same time the process turned out to be simple enough and well-guided by the tool to be usable for a small or medium enterprise (SME) such as BOC.

Since the current version of the DSS (Venues 4Clouds) is at prototype stage only, both the data gathered about Cloud providers and the pool of assets and risks already predefined in the tool are in no way complete at the time of writing. Provided that the systems knowledgebase will grow over time and that the data available can be maintained up to date and accurate, e.g. by employing self-learning mechanisms and being able to extract data from multiple online sources, it will be able to assist SMEs such as BOC in continuously keeping track of a large number of potential providers and in analysing them in a cost efficient way.

13.3.2 Application Deployment to Multiple Clouds

Before the start of the MODAClouds project BOC already had gathered some experience with deployment automation by employing the configuration management system Puppet to automate software installation in their application hosting environment. However, when it came to deployment to the Cloud and, in particular, to multiple Clouds, they soon realized some shortcomings of their approach:

- Even though Puppet provides configuration modules for different Cloud stacks like e.g. OpenStack, provisioning of IaaS instances in a totally Cloud-stack-independent, transparent way was hard to accomplish.
- Deploying parts of the application (e.g. the database tier) to PaaS would be even harder since it would require the use of another configuration to deploy the application stack to PaaS.

As soon as a first version of MODAClouds design time component CloudML4Clouds which is responsible for deploying the modelled application was available, BOC started evaluating the component and found the following potential benefits:

- It would enable them to automatically deploy to any of the Cloud systems previously selected by Venues 4Clouds including the provisioning of Cloud instances in a transparent way, resulting in a higher degree of automation and consequently less manual operation efforts.
- The model-based nature of the approach was expected to enable BOC to document individual deployments in a traceable and comprehensible way and support them in explaining deployment decisions to their customers.

However, it also turned out that using CloudML4Clouds to deploy on Windows Virtual Machines—one of the application components to be deployed in BOCs case is a Windows application—had some disadvantages compared to the use of Linux based VMs. In particular, the tool is relying on the Windows Remote Management protocol to execute remote commands and to deploy to a Windows VM which in turn requires CloudML4Clouds to be executed on a Windows machine. BOC had already invested in developing scripts for Puppet deploying parts of their application to Windows and preferred to capitalize on these investments rather than having to re-implement these scripts using Windows PowerShell commands. Hence, they decided together with the partners involved in developing the component to start an initiative to integrate CloudML4Clouds with Puppet modules.

At the time of writing all required extensions needed for deploying software components through Puppet on Windows VMs are available and BOC currently evaluates the usability of the Puppet extension to CloudML [8].

Since Puppet and similar tools like Chef are widely used in the DevOps community BOC expects the possibility to integrate them with CloudML4Clouds to be beneficial for a large number of potential users.

13.3.3 Cloud Application Monitoring

Before deciding to push the SaaS business, BOC already had a basic monitoring solution in place for several hosting projects. It was based on infrastructure performance indicators like CPU load and RAM consumption as well as the basic availability of the customer facing frontends and central backend components. When going larger scale with a full-fledged SaaS platform, the system health and performance need to be tracked more in detail in order to be able to mitigate issues at an early stage. Such a monitoring solution needs to collect application specific data and in some cases combine metrics from various sources in order to provide the comprehensive view of the whole system required by the operations engineers.

This is where MODAClouds' monitoring technology Tower 4Clouds (Chap. 5) has been introduced with great success. Its Resource Description Framework (RDF) based streaming technology together with a flexible approach to configure data collectors and data analysers provide a solid framework for the challenges of a reliable and extensible monitoring platform.

Tower 4Clouds can be used as part of the complete MODAClouds toolset including design time quality constraint modelling, CloudML deployment and runtime self-adaptation. However, the MODAClouds monitoring components can as well become building blocks for tailored environments, even if the other parts of Energizer 4Clouds are not being used. In the case of BOC's SaaS platform it has been integrated with the existing solution based on the open source tool Icinga.[1] This solution allows the operations team to continue working with the well-established Icinga frontend and its service recovery mechanisms while obtaining more details about the state of the platform. Furthermore, MODAClouds' concept for data collectors makes it very easy for the DevOps engineers to extend the number and the types of metrics collected.

The integration of the stream based monitoring framework with the Icinga poll-based metrics acquisition has been implemented by leveraging the observer interface for Tower 4Clouds and providing a generic Icinga plugin for retrieving the collected data from the observer. With such a toolset adding a new metric that can be acquired with an existing data collector is just a matter of extending the data collector's configuration accordingly and defining a corresponding service within Icinga.

An additional benefit from the usage of MODAClouds' technology for monitoring is that all streams that represent numeric time-series data can be also directed into the Metrics Explorer (see Chap. 5), a web based graphing tool. This can be very useful for the operations engineers when a retrospective view at system performance indicators is needed and trends are to be interpolated.

The monitoring solution architecture for BOC's SaaS platform based on Tower 4Clouds, Icinga and the Metrics Explorer is depicted in Fig. 13.2.

[1] https://www.icinga.org/icinga/icinga-2/distributed-monitoring/.

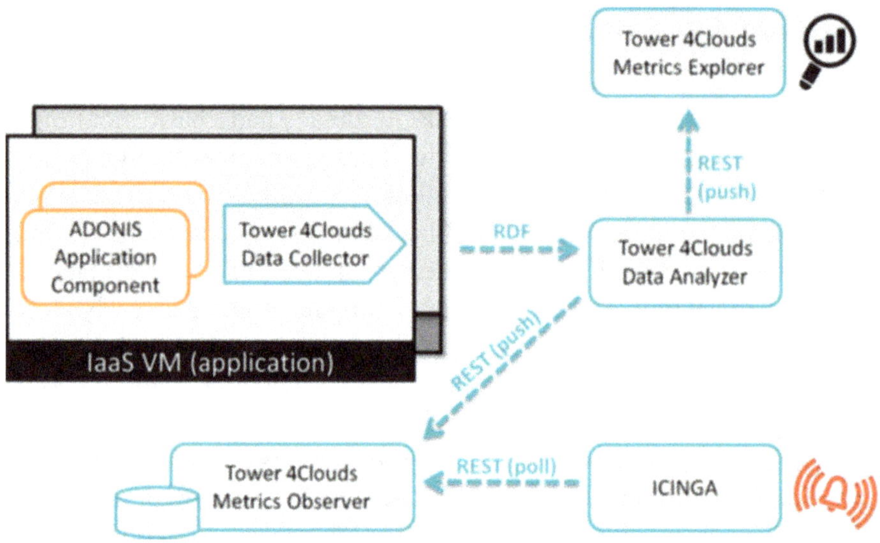

Fig. 13.2 Monitoring solution architecture for BOC's SaaS platform

13.3.4 Cloud to Cloud Migration

One of the key motivations for choosing IaaS technology over other models such as housing is the shift from capital expenditure (CAPEX) to operational expenditure (OPEX). This enables service providers to relocate their services among multiple infrastructures without losing investments. For BOC's Cloud services this capability is an essential asset as it allows for cost optimisation and it also can be the right approach for dealing with availability or performance issues encountered within a specific infrastructure. In addition there is another valid use case for Cloud-to-Cloud migration: customers especially in the public administration sector are confronted with changing regulatory policies related to location of services and data they use for their work. Such policies may at some point in time prohibit usage of services and storage of data outside the respective country.

BOC's SaaS platform has been designed with the objective to be extensible to sites located in different countries if customers have the need to have their data stored and services deployed in specific geographical locations. This is achieved by relying on basic IaaS for compute, storage and network resources managed through CloudML which in turn triggers Puppet [9] for deploying and configuring the BOC services. This Cloud vendor independent toolchain enables BOC to move their services among IaaS platforms from various providers.

The Cloud-to-Cloud migration approach chosen by BOC is one that relies on data replication mechanisms of the used database management system (MS SQL Server or Oracle Database), CloudML for deploying application stacks in multiple sites and the REST-enabled MODAClouds load balancer for switching the traffic from one site to the other. The complete procedure that needs to be executed to perform the switch from site A to site B consists of the following steps.

1. Create a deployment model for site B including a load balancer instance pointing at site A and B application stacks as well as a DBMS instance. Update the deployment model for site A adding the application stack of site B to the load balancer.
2. Enact the deployment one both sites with CloudML, them create a full database backup on site A and restore it on site B.
3. Update the deployment model of site A to remove the application stack. Enact the change of site A with CloudML (start of downtime). Create a differential database backup on site A and restore it on site B.
4. Update the deployment model for site B adding the application stack. Enact the deployment change on site B with CloudML (end of downtime). Trigger the DNS switch for the publicly accessible domain so that the user traffic is routed to the load balancer on site B.
5. Once all traffic is on site B update the deployment model on site A removing the DBMS and the load balancer as well as all underlying IaaS resources. Release all resources on site A by enacting the deployment model with CloudML.

The main steps of the relocation are depicted in Fig. 13.3.

As all of the involved steps are scriptable, automation is possible if the frequency of the migration use case justifies the effort for implementing the automated solution based on the procedure described above.

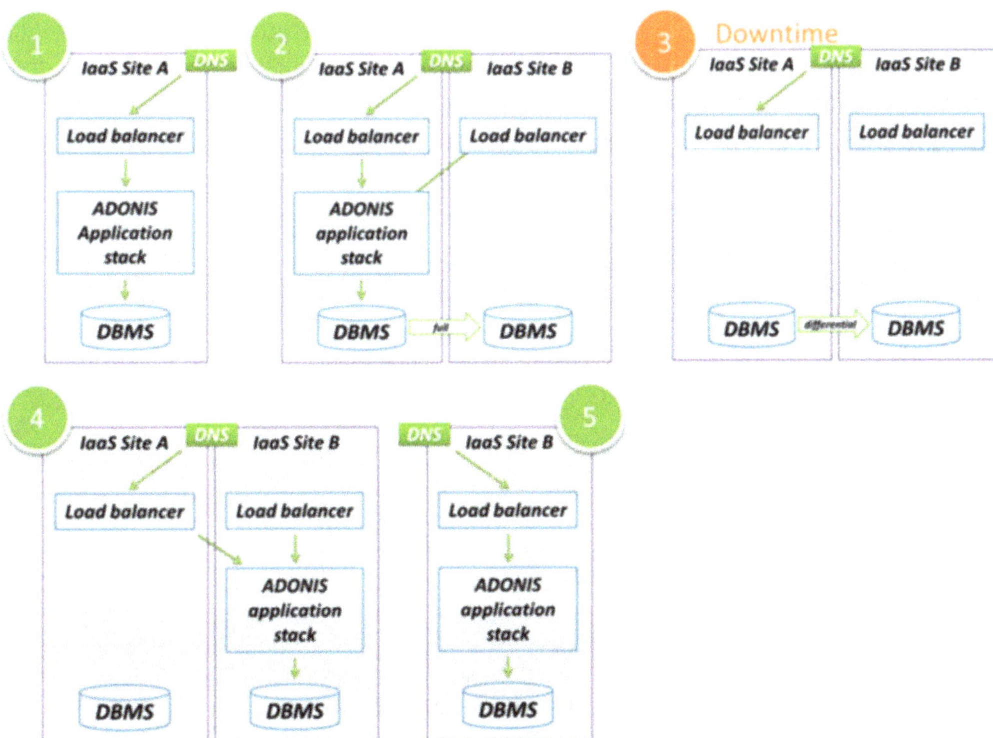

Fig. 13.3 Main steps of the Cloud-to-Cloud relocation

13.4 Conclusion and General Recommendations

Even though some of the experiences and observations made are specific to the case described in this chapter, the authors believe that some general recommendations can be derived for companies or, more specifically, SMEs that are either planning to cloudify some of their business critical software or, being a software provider such as BOC, to extend their business model with an SaaS offering.

As mentioned earlier there are several good reasons to think about Cloud application monitoring as well as a strategy to migrate from one Cloud provider to another from the very beginning of the Cloud migration process. This should encompass the following aspects:

- When selecting a particular Cloud service, the ease of migration to another equivalent service should be considered. This implies on one hand the existence of such services and on the other hand the ability to migrate software components and data to these other services easily.
- In order to increase cost efficiency and quality of service the Cloud service provider market should be analysed on a regular basis. The selection of Cloud services and Cloud providers might become a reoccurring task. A common knowledge base and a tool based approach for decision making as planned for MODAClouds Venues 4Clouds tool will help saving efforts for data acquisition and analysis and making decisions in a traceable, comprehensible way.
- In order to be able to easily deploy to different providers deployment automation or even self-adaptation should be considered to save operation efforts. Automated deployment should ideally work on different Cloud stacks (i.e. on different Cloud services) with as little adaptations as possible.
- Monitoring should be considered an integral part of the Cloud service as it is the only reliable way to track SLA adherence. The solution should be easy to use, maintain, extend and at best it shall be managed together with the business application by means of the configuration management system. The combination of an established product such as Icinga with the sophisticated Tower 4Clouds RDF stream processing toolkit is a good candidate for this challenge.

References

1. Alexander Gunka SS (2013). Moving an application to the cloud—an evolutionary approach. In: MultiCloud'13. Prague, Czech Republic
2. BOC (2014) BOC Group: ADONIS:cloud Landing page. Retrieved May 2015, from http://www.boc-group.com/at/adoniscloud (2015). Retrieved May 2015, from https://www.icinga.org/
3. Smrati Gupta VMM (2015, May 5–7). Risk-driven Framework for Decision Support in Cloud Service Selection. In: 15th IEEE/ACM International Symposium on Cluster, Cloud and Grid Computing (CC-GRID (2015) Shenzhen. Guangdong, China
4. MODAClouds (2013) Deliverable 2.3.1: decision making toolkit requirements and architecture, and update on business methodology. Retrieved May 2015, from MODAClouds: http://www.modaclouds.eu/publications/public-deliverables/

5. Omerovic A, Muntes MV (2013) Towards a method for decision support in multi-cloud environments. In: Proceedings Fourth International Conference on Cloud Computing, Grids, and Virtualization (CLOUD COMPUTING 2013) pp 162–180
6. Muntes Mulero VPM (n.d.) Eliciting risk, quality and cost aspects in multi-cloud environments. In: Proceedings Fourth International Conference on Cloud Computing, Grids, and Virtualization (CLOUD COMPUTING 2013) pp 238–243
7. MODAClouds (2014) Deliverable 2.3.2: decision making toolkit requirements and architecture, and update on business methodology. Appendix A. Retrieved May 2015, from MODAClouds: http://www.modaclouds.eu/wp-content/uploads/2012/09/MODAClouds/_D2.3.2/_-DecisionMakingToolkitRequirementsAndArchitectureAndUpdateOnBusinessMethodology.pdf
8. MODAClouds (2015) D4.3.3 MODACloudML IDE—final version. Retrieved May 2015, from http://www.modaclouds.eu/wp-content/uploads/2012/09/MODAClouds_D4.3.3_MODACloudMLIDEFinalVersion.pdf
9. Puppet (2015) Puppet. Retrieved May 2015, from https://puppetlabs.com

Chapter 14
Healthcare Application

Francesco D'andria and Roi Sucasas Font

14.1 Introduction

This chapter presents a real life case based on a case study from Atos which uses the MODAClouds framework to manage the design, deployment and governance of a telemedicine solution in a hybrid multi-Cloud environment.

The Atos eHealth telemedicine solution is a software application, based on the state-of-the-art in ICT that aims at developing an innovative and integrated solution for the general management of patients suffering from dementia. It provides an integrated online clinical, educational, and social network to support dementia sufferers and also their caregivers. Based on a set of monitoring parameters and measuring scales, this solution aims to early detect symptoms that predict decline, avoid emergencies and secondary effects and, ultimately, prolong the period that patients can remain safely cared at home, no matter where it is located. There are various stakeholders involved in this scenario that would benefit from the system capabilities offered by the eHealth application:

Patients and their caregivers:

- Access to services, like videos or games, recommended by clinicians or experts.
- Collect and register data and measurements (blood pressure, weight, activity levels, questionnaires, etc.).
- Management of warnings or requests sent to the clinicians.

R.S. Font (✉)
ATOS Spain SA, Subida al Mayorazgo, 24B Planta 1, 38110 Santa Cruz de Tenerife, Spain
e-mail: roi.sucasas@atos.net

F. D'andria
ATOS Spain SA, Av. Diagonal, 200, 08011 Barcelona, Spain
e-mail: francesco.dandria@atos.net

E. Di Nitto et al. (eds.), *Model-Driven Development and Operation of Multi-Cloud Applications*, PoliMI SpringerBriefs,
DOI 10.1007/978-3-319-46031-4_14

- Improve awareness on the use of their sensitive data, like the patients monitoring parameters and the patients medication follow-up and drug adverse events.

Clinicians and Health System (organization of people, institutions and resources to deliver health care)

- Continuous monitoring and follow-up of the patients
- Management and assignment of tasks and questionnaires
- Services to meet the health needs of target populations
- Improve workload of assistance teams:
- Institutions/specialists dynamically added and removed on demand
- Allocation/De-allocation of Cloud resources depending on the workload.
- Rapid elasticity, i.e., the network can respond rapidly and automatically to changes in demand from particular doctor/specialist
- Improve access to and participation in the Knowledge and Information Society for citizens
- help monitoring of risks like: data breaches/inappropriate access, disruption of service and data)

Originally a monolithic web application, this new telemedicine solution has been re-designed for a multi-Cloud environment. This software solution that consists of two main software blocks: a multi-Cloud server-side block and a client-side block. The server-side block consists of a database and two server applications. All of them can be deployed in different multi-Cloud scenarios alternatives, like private Clouds, public Clouds or hybrid scenarios. The client-side block consists of a desktop application (used by the patients and their caregivers) that connects to one of the server applications.

14.2 EHealth Cloud Solution: Why to Deploy It in a Multi-Cloud Environment?

There are many real and potential benefits of a multi-Cloud based telemedicine solution. This section describes these benefits (also the cons and risks associated to this approach) from two different points of view: the application (including designers, developers, and administrators), and the final users (the patients and their caregivers, and the doctors).

Because of the number of users of this application, the amount of database transactions, and also the load and traffic conditions that can vary significantly, it is not trivial to accurately estimate the resources required by this solution. To be able to scale the resources on demand is one of the main advantages of a multi-Cloud approach. The Cloud providers allow us to administer these challenges in an easy way, also reducing costs and management times. This reduced technical maintenance (that also applies to the deployment and the backup and recovery tasks) is also a feature that will be very useful in this case study. Another important characteristic of the eHealth solution is the capability of integrating and connecting multiple third party tools or services.

This will allow us to scale the functionalities and features offered at a much lower cost compared with an own development and a later deployment in a private / public infrastructure. For example the eHealth GUI component could be deployed in a public PaaS or IaaS, making use of third party services offered by these providers, like email delivery services, monitoring services etc. This approach would safe us money and time, and would also allow an easier growth of the application's functionalities and capabilities in the future. The developers wont need to create new applications from scratch with the same functionalities offered by these third party services. A multi-Cloud environment also offers us flexibility, for example it will allow us to easily move components from one provider to another when needed. Also the final users of this solution can benefit from it. The deployment of the eHealth solution in a multi-Cloud environment will make it possible to access it from everywhere. Patients and caregivers will connect from home with clinicians. This will facilitate the home health monitoring and follow-up of these users by the clinicians. Patients and their caregivers will send them different kind of measurements (activity, weight, blood pressure, etc.) and tests results, so that doctors can make a diagnostic with all these data. Also the eHealth solution will analyze these data in order to detect early deterioration symptoms. Patients with dementia wont need to go to hospital so frequently, and doctors can make a better and individualized follow up of them. It is expected that this set of tools and features will reduce the workload of these clinicians, and will also reduce the costs of the health system. And from the point of view of the patients and caregivers, its also expected that with this direct and frequent connection (and monitoring) with clinicians, their quality of life will be better.

14.3 Risks and Problems

There are some risks associated with this approach. The most important of these risks may be the data and privacy protection and the different legislations of each country associated with the management of this data. The preservation of this medical information and the confidentiality is a major challenge in all telemedicine systems. Another very common risk in Cloud computing is the vendor lock-in. PaaS and IaaS providers are heterogeneous and the provided features are often incompatible. This can be a serious inconvenience in such a multi-Cloud approach. These providers present another problem: which ones are the best for our case study? Not only may the prices of the different providers vary, but also their availability and the offered services. In order to deploy all the eHealth components in a multi-Cloud environment, a great knowledge of the available Cloud providers will be needed. Other risks associated to this kind of telemedicine solutions are the availability and reliability of their services. In emergency cases, the access to these services can mean the difference between life and death. In particular, in those emergencies where a fast medical response time is needed, the availability of these services can be critical. The database and other components of the eHealth solution shall be accessible without interruption 24 × 7. This could become a problem because its very important to continue monitoring not only the health of these business-critical applications but also their performance. In order to monitor these properties and also the performance of each of the components, it will be needed to use some kind of monitoring application that could react to issues related to them. Moreover, to define a set of rules, constraints or SLAs for the eHealth application components should be a mandatory requirement.

14.4 EHealth and MODAClouds: The Story

At this point, Juan, the responsible (administrator, designer and developer) of the eHealth solution, wants to use the MODAClouds platform to be able to design, deploy, monitor and manage this telemedicine application on a hybrid PaaS environment. Why MODAClouds? He expects to take advantage of all the Cloud environment benefits described before and at the same time he expects to solve most of the problems and risks of such approach. MODAClouds offers a set of tools for the design and run time. On one hand the design-time tools offer the capability of designing a Cloud agnostic model of the solution, the capability of defining the QoS/SLA rules that will be used during the run-time, and also the capability of avoiding the vendor lock-in by providing a list of all available Cloud providers, that match the eHealth technical and business requirements, where this solution could be deployed. On the other hand the run-time tools will monitor the different solution components and will react properly to these monitoring values by scaling the components up or down, or by migrating the components from one provider to another. This is the theory. Juan will prove it soon. Juan will use two different PaaS providers accounts: one in Pivotal (a public PaaS provider based on Cloud Foundry) and another in a private Cloud Foundry server with few resources available. He thinks that hosting the database and the web services application in this private PaaS will make it possible to handle some of the data and privacy protection risks mentioned before. It will allow him to restrict and control in an efficient way the access to the data that is stored there. Only the web services application (the application that handles the connections with the database) will be able to access the content of this database. But because he thinks that this is not enough, the critical data will also be encrypted by this web service application. This way the same application that handles the access to the database will be the responsible of encrypting the data. This application is also responsible of managing the roles and permissions of the users that want to access the content of the database by accepting or refusing the requests depending on the users roles. He also thinks that deploying the other eHealth component (Web GUI application) in the private server could be the best option for a first moment, where only a limited set of users will make use of the eHealth solution. Once the application starts to grow in number of users and starts to have difficulties in handling the incoming traffic, he could migrate some components from the private Cloud to a public Cloud. But instead of migrating the components manually, Juan will use MODAClouds to define a set of rules and SLAs so that the MODAClouds run-time components can do that in an automatic way. In order to achieve all this, Juan will follow the steps described below.

Cloud agnostic solution design and Cloud provider selection

First, Juan uses Creator4Clouds to do a Cloud agnostic model of the eHealth solution. This is the model of the components that will be deployed in the Cloud without specifying where and how they will be deployed. These components are the following: the main database, the web services application and the Web GUI application. For each of these components he defines the provided and required interfaces, which are needed to define the connections between each component and are also needed to define the methods or components that will be monitored. After refining all these models, the next step is to get a list of all available PaaS providers that match the functional and business requirements. Juan wants to know which the best options for this solution are. On one hand he needs to host in a private Cloud the database and the web services application. This way he can preserve the data and privacy protection. The other component, the web GUI application (called eHealth-gui in the models), can be deployed either in a private or in a public Cloud. Juan uses the Venues 4Clouds tool in order to get all the providers that match his business and functional requirements. As a result of this he gets Pivotal / Cloud Foundry as the best choice (in terms of costs, services offered, etc.).

Now Juan wants to define how the MODAClouds run-time tools will behave once the application components are deployed in the selected provider.

Modelling of the QoS and SLAs

In order to do that, Juan continues using the Creator 4Clouds tool to define the Quality of Service constraints and penalties that will be used by the MODAClouds run-time tools. He wants to monitor the performance of the application components. To do that he defines two constraints: Response Time (to check the response time of some operations) and Throughput (to check requests per second). These two constraints will be used to monitor the traffic and performance of the deployed web applications.

He uses the interfaces defined before to associate these constraints to the interface or to some of its methods. He decides that if theres too much traffic (by specifying a value in the Throughput constraint), the SLA tool should migrate the Web GUI application to a public PaaS. To define this behavior, he associates this constraint to a penalty (called Migrate Penalty). This way, once the number of users grows, both applications will have more resources to be scaled up. Also the SLA tool would send events (i.e. emails) to Juan if some other SLA violation occurs. This migration penalty or behavior could also be defined by using other MODAClouds tools. Creator 4Clouds will then transform these constraints and penalties models to generate the monitoring rules and penalties used by the Tower 4Clouds and the SLA tool during the run-time.

The data collector library

Juan will need to connect the deployed eHealth components with Tower 4Clouds, the MODAClouds monitoring tool. First Juan imports the data collector library (a remote component of the Tower 4Clouds tool) in the application, then he configures it, and finally he generates the packed files that will be deployed (.war files). But before deploying them, Juan needs to finish the models.

Refining the models

Before deploying the eHealth application, Juan needs to do a few more things. On one hand he associates the model components with the 'physical' applications. In the case of the eHealth cloud components, the 'physical' applications are packed in two .war files: one for each of the java web server applications. And on the other hand he specifies the cloud providers where these components will be deployed. At this point the eHealth application components are ready to be deployed.

EHealth deployment

Once Juan has modelled all the components, including all the QoS constraints and SLAs, its time to deploy them in the private Cloud Foundry server. The Creator 4Clouds tool offers the option of generating different models for different providers. But for now, Juan only creates one model for deploying the application components in the private Cloud Foundry. To do that, Creator 4Clouds connects with CloudML4Clouds, which is the responsible of deploying the application components in the selected providers. Juan selects the deploy option and waits until the application is deployed and ready. Then it starts the application execution and makes it available to his customers.

Run-time tools: Check the status of the application components

Juan accesses the private Cloud Foundry to see that the applications are deployed and running as expected. Then he connects with the Tower 4Clouds and SLA web tools to see if they are correctly connected with the application components. He does a few tests with the eHealth component and checks that all of them are working fine. After Juan checks that the eHealth solution cloud components are deployed and running in the private Cloud Foundry server, he tells his bosses that the application is ready to be used.

14.5 Conclusions

As we could see in this chapter, a multi-cloud approach offers several new possibilities and advantages for telemedicine applications, but it also presents some risks and disadvantages. As was shown in the "real life case", by using the MODAClouds ecosystem, our main character was able of taken benefit of the advantages of such approach, and at the same time, he could avoid most of the risks and disadvantages associated to a multi-cloud deployment.

References

1. Deliverable 4.3.3 MODACloudML IDE final version
2. Deliverable 2.3.2 decision making toolkit requirements and architecture, and update on business methodology
3. Deliverable 7.1.2 case studies requirements—Final version
4. Deliverable 8.1 case study design analysis
5. Deliverable 8.4.2 Healthcare application design—Final prototype design
6. Deliverable 9.3.2 prototype of healthcare application final release

Chapter 15
Operation Control Interfaces

Craig Sheridan and Darren Whigham

15.1 Introduction

An interesting commercial use-case for Flexiant of the MODAClouds solution is based upon adding extra functionality to Flexiant Cloud Orchestrator (FCO) [1] Triggers [2]. Triggers are functions that allow an action in FCO to initiate a second action, which can either be internal or even external to Flexiant Cloud Orchestrator.

A trigger is simply a block of Flexiant Development Language (FDL) [3] code, which is a Lua [4] based language, that is used to extend Flexiant Cloud Orchestrator.Triggers will run either before an event occurs (a pre trigger) or after an event occurs (a post trigger) which can be used to perform a variety of actions such as automatically starting servers at creation time or mailing and alerting based on customer actions.

15.2 Language for Triggers Description

A trigger is written as a block of Flexiant Development Language (FDL) code, which is a Lua based language used to extend Flexiant Cloud Orchestrator. FDL is written as a code block and run within the platform itself. Within FDL there are multiple APIs [5] that can be called such as billing, trigger, and payment. For this chapter we will focus on the trigger API. Triggers can be used to perform any of the following actions:

C. Sheridan · D. Whigham (✉)
Flexiant, London, UK
e-mail: dwhigham@flexiant.com

C. Sheridan
e-mail: csheridan@flexiant.com

E. Di Nitto et al. (eds.), *Model-Driven Development and Operation of Multi-Cloud Applications*, PoliMI SpringerBriefs,
DOI 10.1007/978-3-319-46031-4_15

- Sending email as a result of an action or state change
- Making an HTTP call and processing the result
- Making user API or admin API calls from within FCO.
- Writing an entry in the syslog
- Running a local executable file
- Reading or writing to a file
- Manipulating XML documents, objects, and nodes

To achieve these different actions, various trigger types are utilised. The following table lists these different 'triggerTypes', as well as whether the trigger is initiated before (PRE) or after (POST) the initiating event.

15.3 Architecture of the Trigger Support

The FDL Trigger API, named "TRIGGER", is activated when the user returns from an entry point with the API set to TRIGGER. This makes the entry point a trigger. Once an entry point has been set to act as a trigger, it will return three pieces of additional data when describing themselves; triggerType, triggerOptions, and value object.

The triggerType is the type of event that will initiate the trigger, for example an API call or a change in resource state. This can be refined using the triggerOption object, which is a list stating the specific events that can initiate the trigger. For example, if the triggerType indicates that the trigger can be initiated by a server state change, the triggerOptions determine which server states initiate the trigger.

The value object has the same layout as in the API (See SOAP Value). Each value object specifies a configurable value, together with its validator, thus setting out the permissible values for it.

With all FDL APIs, including TRIGGER, anything which a user prints (to STDOUT or STDERR) will go to the Jade sysout log. The user can log any string to the normal log with logger (which takes a string). If the Lua throws an exception, Jade will catch it. However, the user should aim not to throw exceptions but instead return something appropriate depending on the API.

The entry point will always be called with a single parameter p dependent on the API being called, or a value of nil. If a value other than nil is passed, the return value of the function depends upon the API. In this case, the function is expected to return a table that describes itself. This table will contain the following keys:

- *api*: the name of the API as a string (for instance "BILLING")
- *version*: the version of the API as a number.
- *ref*: a unique identifier for the function. Do not use identifiers starting with an underscore; these are reserved for Flexiant.
- *name*: a string containing the name of the entry point (max 50 characters)
- *description*: a string containing a description of the entry point (maximum 250 characters)

- *execution function*: a reference to a LUA function which is the function to call with values of p other than nil. If this is not specified or is specified as nil, then the same function will be called.

15.4 Usage of Triggers to Enable Load Balancing

Triggers are most commonly used to access all the functionality that is offered by FCO, but they can also be used to make external API calls. Trigger functionality has been added as part of the MODAClouds project to extend the platform and tools capabilities. Within the MODAClouds project a number of unique triggers have been developed.

The first of these triggers is called the Auto Server Failover trigger, which is called should a server be shutdown or killed within a certain customers account.

Upon being called this trigger looks for a Live Server tag attached to the server, and if found, replaces it with a Backup server tag. This new tag can be anything, such as Faulty Server, but for this example Backup server will be used. The trigger then looks in the FCO account for a VM tagged Backup server that is in a stopped state and starts it. Finally, once the new server is started, the Backup server tag is removed and a Live server tag is added.

Another trigger that has been created for the MODAClouds project is the Auto Alert Mail trigger. This will send an email to the account owner to alert them that a server has stopped or been killed. The Auto Alert Mail trigger works by looking for an "Auto Mail" tag assigned to the relevant account whenever FCO registers that a server has been shutdown or killed. This tag contains the recipient address to send an email to, and once found, the trigger sends a message to the address to inform the account holder that a server has been shut down. The message includes the UUID [6] of the server and the Date/time stamp for when this server was shutdown. This useful trigger therefore allows account owners to be notified of any issues with their servers, as well as recording a date/timestamp within the syslog to allow for troubleshooting.

Both of the Auto Server Failover and Auto Mail Alert triggers have been combined and included within the MODAclouds solution as detailed in the following section.

Within the Modacloud project, these triggers have been implemented to work in conjunction with load balancers. As detailed in Fig. 15.1.

The Load Balancer will be set up within the FCO Cloud platform. Behind this will be a number of VM's that will serve load balancers. These VMs will be tagged within FCO as either a Live Server or a Backup Server In the event of an error with these servers that cannot be resolved internally, the server is then shutdown. When this shutdown occurs then the triggers created.

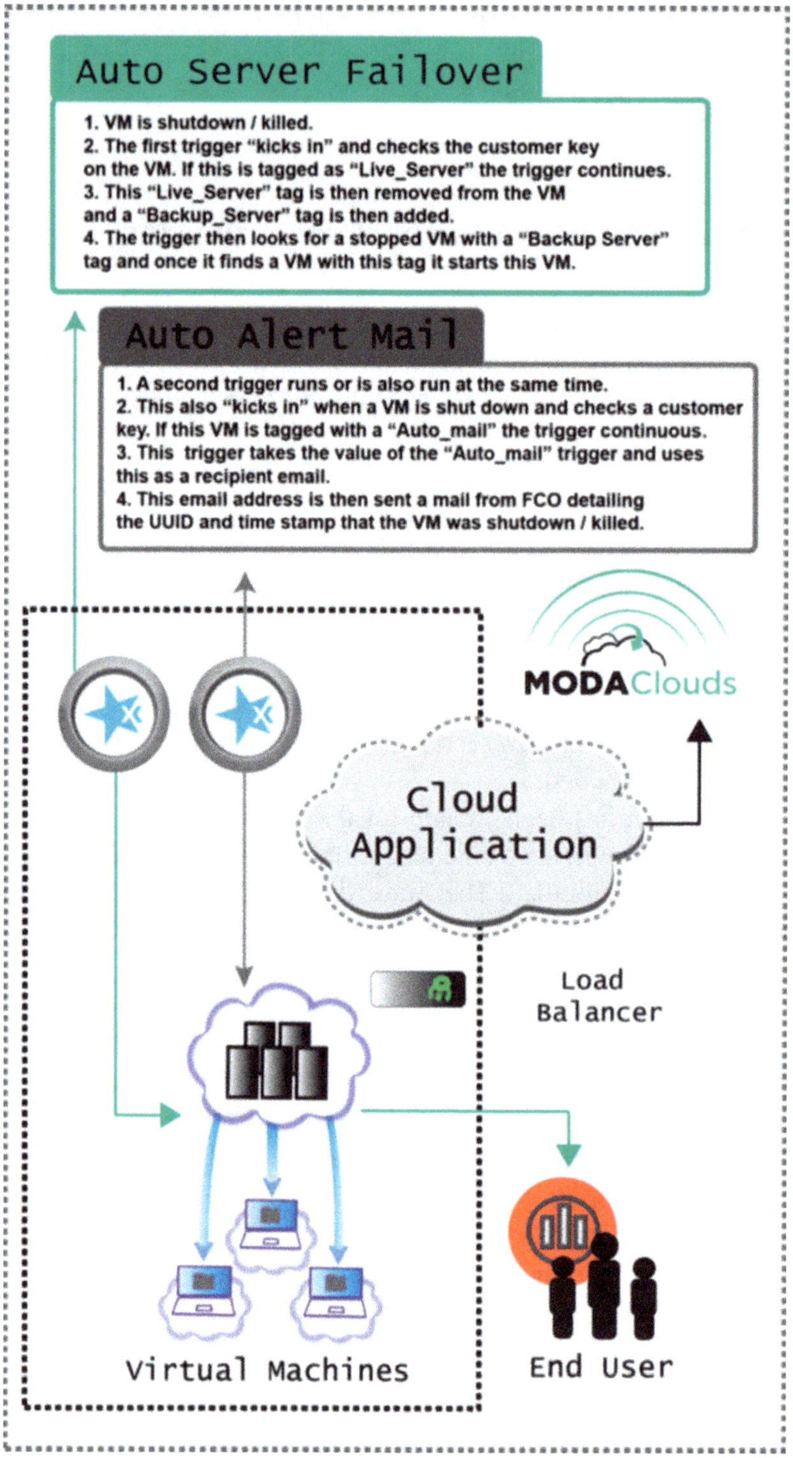

Fig. 15.1 MODAcloud triggers

15.5 Related Work

To be able to monitor and provide similar solutions that are presented here with other Cloud providers external tools/programs using the Cloud providers APIs must be used. To be able to match this functionality providers such as OnApp, VMWare and OpenStack would have to look at using external API calls.

Within FCO and with the use of Triggers and FDL, FCO allows the ability to run and monitor from within the platform rather than using external applications to query using the API. The key benefit of this from a Cloud provider is the reduction in the number of external API calls and the functionality works regardless of the hypervisor/storage/network model underneath.

15.6 Conclusions

This chapter has provided an overview of the trigger technology developed by Flexiant for use within the MODAClouds project. It has showcased the practical use of this service within a real world example and the importance of such technology within the MODAClouds solution. Detailed is the technology underpinning the triggers technology and example triggers created that are freely available and open sourced.

References

1. Flexiant (2015) Software Features Tour. https://www.flexiant.com/flexiant-cloud-orchestrator/
2. Flexiant (2015) 3rd Party Plugins. https://www.flexiant.com/plugins/about-plugins/
3. Flexiant (2016) Flexiant Cloud Orchestrator Developer Guide. http://docs.flexiant.com/display/DOCS/Flexiant+Cloud+Orchestrator+Developer+Guide
4. Ierusalimschy R, de Figueiredo LH, Celes W (2006) Lua 5.1 Reference Manual. http://www.lua.org/manual/5.1/
5. Flexiant (2016) Introduction to Jade APIs. http://docs.flexiant.com/display/DOCS/Introduction+to+Jade+APIs
6. IETF (2005) A Universally Unique IDentifier (UUID) URN Namespace. https://www.ietf.org/rfc/rfc4122.txt

Chapter 16
Conclusion and Future Research

Arnor Solberg and Peter Matthews

16.1 Summary

The MODAClouds approach offers a set of innovative techniques for development and runtime operation management of multicloud applications. In particular it delivers an open source integrated development environment for the high-level design, cloud service selection, early prototyping, QoS assessments, semi-automatic code generation, and automatic deployment of multicloud applications, as presented in Part I Dev. Secondly it delivers a run-time environment for monitoring, dynamic adaptation, and data migration to optimize multicloud application execution with respect to quality of service concerns, as presented in Part II Ops. Thirdly it delivers DevOps enabling features supporting continuous design, deployment and QoS analysis for performance optimization, as presented in Part III DevOps. Finally to demonstrate the technology the book discusses a set of applications from various domains ranging from more classical information systems with the model management and business process modelling applications to the Internet of Things and Cyber Physical Systems domains with e-health and smart city applications. Part IV Applications discusses the demonstration of the general applicability the MODAClouds approach and the main MODAClouds techniques and features, as presented in Part IV Applications.

A. Solberg (✉)
Stiftelsen SINTEF, Postboks 4760 Sluppen, 7465 Trondheim, Norway
e-mail: Arnor.Solberg@sintef.nopleaseaddhere

P. Matthews (✉)
CA Technologies UK, Ditton Park, Riding Court Road, Datchet SL3 9LL, UK
e-mail: peter.matthews@ca.com

E. Di Nitto et al. (eds.), *Model-Driven Development and Operation of Multi-Cloud Applications*, PoliMI SpringerBriefs,
DOI 10.1007/978-3-319-46031-4_16

16.2 Outlook and Further Research

While the MODACLouds approach addresses a set of concerns for multicloud application development and operation, many challenging concerns remain, and new concern arise as new opportunities are discovered in the pace of the continuously evolving digitalized world.

A trend is that *increasingly large and complex systems and systems of systems need to be executed, managed and evolved on hybrid infrastructures* consisting of a continuum of cloud, fog, Cyber Physical Systems and Internet of Things resources and devices. Coping with this continuum represent daunting challenges. These challenges also embrace dealing with "old" concerns but in an even larger scale and in new contexts, for example, seamless management of vast heterogeneity, QoS guarantees and optimization of such complex systems, security, privacy and vulnerability control etc.

A recent trend related to multicloud is federated clouds, where the cloud federation can consist of multiple clouds. MODAClouds provides baseline technologies to support this. Moreover, there is an acknowledgement that the centralized cloud model (all the data are computed and processed centrally in the cloud) that have been the dominating cloud application model until now, does not meet significant requirements such as response time and efficient resource exploitation. A *decentralized cloud model* where computation and processing are also performed at the edges (i.e., fog computing) and the optimal utilization of tiny devices, e.g., for real time response, require new methods and techniques for development and operation.

Preparing the cloud to improve the management of big data and machine learning are challenges that will require *cloud architectures to evolve in the areas of cloud networking, deployment practices and run-time management as well as managing security and privacy needs*. Networking and deployment practices will support an agile and DevOps approach to application requirements fulfillment.

DevOps is part of a strategy that will lead to continuous delivery, the frequent updates and bug fixes that are characteristic of the best apps in the mobile arena. This project has shown that creating applications from previously composed services will shorten the delivery time. The use of SLA monitoring and automated deployment also embrace a DevOps strategy. Cloud services that have to be unit tested after change and composed into an application that can have automated or semi-automated integration testing again shortens the application supply chain. All of these support a DevOps approach, however, there needs to be more work done on increasing the automated supply chain to include integration testing, requirements management and composition.

An additional area that will require further work is in the *security domain*. Whenever cloud computing adoption is discussed there are many commentators and users who claim that the cloud is insecure. This is now being countered by the realization that most of the security and vulnerability issues are the same issues for IT in general. There are no authentication issues that are present in cloud computing architectures such as SaaS and PaaS that are not there in general non-cloud applications. The addition of multi cloud applications where federations of cloud services, containers and microservices are orchestrated or tightly bound into applications brings some interesting challenges. Since many of these services are not fully under the developers control, being accessed only by APIs there is an increased risk to an application. A composed or orchestrated application is only as secure as the least secure component. It is important in an increasingly agile development world that the security metrics of a service are well understood and reported. Making note of liability exclusions in an SLA, even if its not in small print, is of no comfort to an organization who has been penetrated via an insecure service. This is well recognised and is being addressed in a number of research programs, not the least the MUSA project. This project is targetted at the above security issues and will extend the MODAClouds DSS to enable the selection and runtime monitoring of service security performance as well as risk, cost etc., that are part of the MODAClouds project. There are other proposals as well as funded research in the area of regulatory compliance, assurance etc. that are addressing the security gaps in cloud and particularly multicloud applications. This area will become increasingly important as more public services become available, delivering government, finance and healthcare data to the application developers and user.

www.ingramcontent.com/pod-product-compliance
Lightning Source LLC
LaVergne TN
LVHW082236200926
848484LV00008B/2364
* 9 7 8 1 0 1 3 2 6 7 9 3 2 *